TEN THOUSAND GOODBYES

*Lifetime Reflections
of a
Traveling Man*

ROBERT M. MORGAN

ON THE COVER ~

Sternwheel Steamboat Henderson *~ one of her final roles of steamboater elegance, as the glory days of steamboating neared their end, placed in competition against the much newer, steel-hulled* Portland *came about in 1952. They vied on the Columbia River abreast of Morgan's Landing Farm's shoreline in the "Last Great Sternwheel Steamboat Race." The race was billed to commemorate the first showing of "Bend in the River," starring Jimmy Stewart. The* Henderson*, re-named for the movie as the* River Queen*, was also a star. Years before her movie role, her single cylinder engines had been converted to tandem compound with the additions of low pressure cylinders. Her additional power turning her huge sternwheel at a smart 30 revolutions per minute, captained by the prowess of Captain Sidney J. "Happy" Harris, gave the sentimental boat speed to win that final race.*

TEN THOUSAND GOODBYES

Lifetime Reflections
of a
Traveling Man

ROBERT M. MORGAN

P Premiere Editions International, Inc.
Corvallis, Oregon

Also by Robert M. Morgan . . .
WATER AND THE LAND
A HISTORY OF AMERICAN IRRIGATION

PREMIERE EDITIONS INTERNATIONAL, INC.
2397 NW Kings Blvd #311, Corvallis, OR 97330
TELEPHONE: (541) 752-4239 ~ FAX: (541) 752-4463
E-MAIL: *publish@premiere-editions.com*
WEB SITE: *www.premiere-editions.com*

EDITORS: Irene L. Gresick
                              Beatrice Stauss

DESIGNER: Nancy K. Marshall –
                              Marshall Designs

PHOTO EDITOR: Theresa Rolow

WATERCOLOR ARTIST: Randall H. Stauss

Printed in the United States of America
First edition, November 1997
ISBN: 09633818-9-X
Library of Congress Catalog Card Number 97-75415

Dedicated to

Lucy Ann Wendell Morgan

*Like a small reflective crystalline pool, with center bubbling
fountain, goldfish and baby-breath fern, her iridescent surface
shimmers with each invading ray of golden sunlight.*

ACKNOWLEDGMENTS

I gratefully acknowledge valuable assistance, re-print permission, photographs, editorial and artistic contributions from the following: Greg L. Nelson, for research and editorial contributions on the Edward Morgan family; June Sarah Tillman, for her general support and family photographs; James Medford Copeland, for excerpts from his writings, family dates and inspiration; Beatrice Hyland Stauss, for her editing skills and laborious corrections; the Oregon Historical Society, for library excerpts; Jean Fears, editor of the *Sauvie Island Outlook*, for re-print permission; Mabel Howell Dudley, for statistics and dates; Nancy Lipp Wolford, for dates and name verifications; *H. W. McCurdy's, A Marine History of the Northwest,* (Second edition, 1896 to 1965), for dates and details; The Oregon Maritime Center and Museum, for specifics on the sternwheel steam tow boat, *Portland,* the last of her kind; and Randall Hyland Stauss, for the original watercolor painting that appears on the front cover and last page.

Except as otherwise noted, all photographs and illustrations are from my family albums and private files. The sidebar stories, articles and poems are also my own work, created over the years to commemorate significant milestones in my life.

Robert M. Morgan
September 1997

Lucy Ann Wendell
at age 18

Lucy Ann

Good fortune surely smiled on me
That far-off summer day,
The odds were . . . it was meant to be.
I've been a winner, every way,
thanks to her strength and grace.
Who knows what might have been my fate,
Without her trust and taste;
A happy never-ending date.

We started small as most folks do,
That December in thirty-eight.
But once we took off . . . The years just flew
As we learned to associate.
We've rarely seen a gloomy time
In six hundred moons or more,
For married bliss, this one's been fine,
The myriad memories to store.

In half a century . . . Ten thousand goodbyes,
'Twas her lot to endure.
A home to tend, plus the children's lives,
A Godly stance was her cure.
She worked it out a hundred ways.
And so I hail her . . . Dear Heart Number One,
Mother Supreme, is the role she plays.
Life's meter shows, all those decades,
To us, life has just begun.

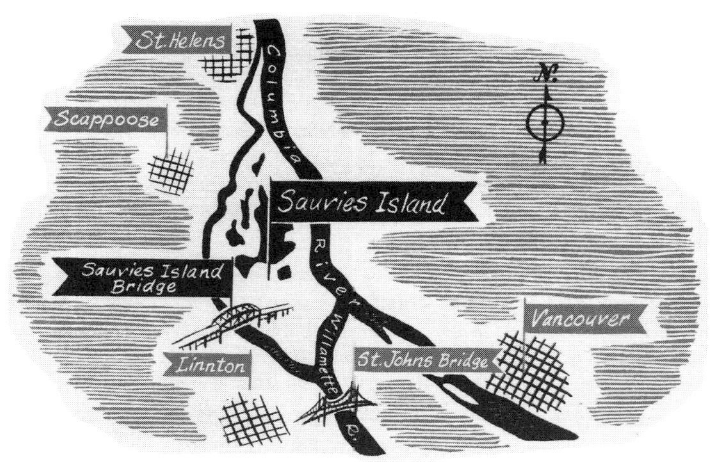

Sauvie Island Bridge spanning the Multnomah Channel, two miles north of Portland, Oregon Courtesy: Sauvie Island Bridge Dedication Program, 1950

TABLE OF CONTENTS

INTRODUCTION .... PAGE 11

THE MORGAN CLAN (POEM) .... PAGE 15

PART ONE:
THE EARLY YEARS................................ PAGE 21

PART TWO:
A LARGER WORLD .... PAGE 61

PART THREE:
THE LONG, WINDING TRAIL~
THE CAREER YEARS .... PAGE 101

PART FOUR:
REFLECTIONS~
HAPPENINGS GREAT AND SMALL................. PAGE 123

SOMETHING OF A
SAUVIE ISLAND LIFE .... PAGE 149
(FOUR SHORT ARTICLES)

A LETTER TO MY SONS .... PAGE 159

EARLY HISTORY OF THE FAMILY OF
EDWARD AND MARY MORGAN .... PAGE 166

QUEEN OF HEARTS (POEM) .... PAGE 173

ABOUT THE AUTHOR .... PAGE 174

*Mother Bessie
Mae Morgan
with Robert,
1914*

INTRODUCTION

*A*lthough not of significant note to the nation as a whole, my birth date was an orientation point of the Century's young second decade in notable ways. It had been a comparatively short span of years since General William T. Sherman of the Union Army had concluded his historic "March To The Sea," a devastating military force that broke the spirit of the shattered Confederate Army. The horrors of the Civil War ended June 1, 1865. That was slightly more than 47 years prior to my March 3, 1913 birth date. Now, at my advancing age, 47 years seems less than an extended period in historical affairs.

I am an admirer today of Theodore Roosevelt, President, 1901-1909 and, among his many, many other achievements, *The Great Champion Of The West*. I arrived as a newborn, eleven short years after "Rough Rider" Roosevelt established the U. S. Bureau of Reclamation, the Federal Agency that bettered the vast American lands west of the Rocky Mountains.

One of my later super attractions, the American automobile, was becoming an industrial force and doing just fine in 1913. A few months prior to my arrival, the first Chevrolet, a classic, large automobile was assembled in Detroit, selling then for the astronomical price of $2,999.00.

Ford's model T was the most popular car in 1913. It would be two years later though when electric headlights first became standard equipment. A used 1924 model T roadster was my first car by necessity. It was the only means by which I could get to high school. I drove seven miles, two through mud and five on a macadam road where I parked, then caught the Burlington Ferry which crossed the Multnomah Channel, then walked to Hadley's store on Highway 30 to catch the school bus to Scappoose High School. As a farm boy, I was impressed with our fine school bus, a new 1926 Dodge one-and-a-half ton chassis with a new 20-passenger body which the owner-driver could remove in summer to install a flat bed for hauling wood and sacked grain.

Automobiles, buses and trucks were of great interest to me. I studied every detail of the vehicles of the mid-twenties. One of great intrigue that I rode on occasionally, that ran from Portland to Astoria on Highway 30, was the Spokane-Portland & Seattle Railway stage. It was a White Motor Company model 54, long wheelbase equipped with a passenger body with right-hand side doors at each row of passenger seats. I also admired with great relish the elegant Pierce-Arrows, Packards, Peerlesses, Premiers, Franklins, Marmons and Rickenbackers, to name a few of the fine machines of the era, all of which have long been gone.

These remarks have come to mind just as orientation, to establish the niche in life that I found myself in during those early formative years.

This and what is to follow have been done in loving tribute to my diverse and dedicated family of children, grandchildren and great-grandchildren.

It is of inestimable satisfaction to Wendy and me to observe the developments, aspirations, triumphs and achievements our offspring have contrived as they have formulated their exciting lives.

Ten Thousand Goodbyes takes me, a "country boy," from soon after the turn of the century through an amalgam of decades that treated me to a chronology of events that afforded me an abundant life of family devotion and love.

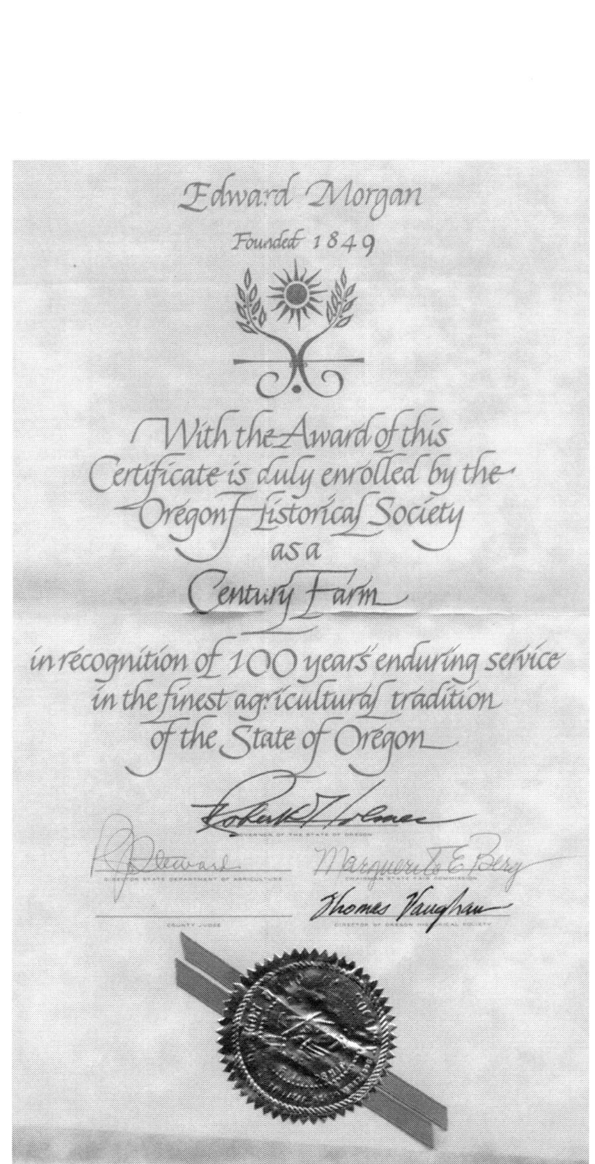

Edward Morgan
Founded 1849
With the Award of this
Certificate is duly enrolled by the
Oregon Historical Society
as a
Century Farm
in recognition of 100 years enduring service
in the finest agricultural tradition
of the State of Oregon
GOVERNOR OF THE STATE OF OREGON
DIRECTOR STATE DEPARTMENT OF AGRICULTURE
CHAIRMAN STATE FAIR COMMISSION
COUNTY JUDGE
DIRECTOR OF OREGON HISTORICAL SOCIETY

THE MORGAN CLAN

The little group met late that night
Their wives served cakes and tea;
They agreed as one to set sails and sights
And cross the shining sea.

Young Ed was there with plans a lot;
His family shared his views.
The MORGAN CLAN, of good Welsh stock,
Was preparing a life, all new.

The promise of a bright fresh land
Braced each and every heart.
They fain could wait to grasp the "brand"
And make this strange strong start.

With minds made up, the die was cast;
America was their goal.
Concluding all of the plans, at last;
All moves were made to go.

Ohio State was Ed's home anew,
His family grew close and strong.
Affairs ran well, he prospered too;
Proud Jayhawks were his throng.

Things seemed just right, then sadness came;
Wife Sarah heard Heaven's call.
All things held dear seemed halt and lame
That heartbreak Wabash fall.

Edward was a vital man,
His stock was firm and strong.
He breached the hurt with God's kind hand.
His little brood too met the loss
Of a mother's love now gone.

The fold cried out for the womanly touch,
Kind hands to mold and mind.
The small ones needed a mother to clutch,
And cast their loss behind.

Some time went by, then new love came
To Edward's vibrant soul;
All joined anew to grow, and claim
The MORGAN aims and goal.

Then from somewhere adventure's scent
Again filled Edward's head;
The stories of a "Golden West"
Pulled hard at his pioneer bent.

The vivid call was not denied,
Ed's family planned anew.
All earthly things were cast aside;
Missouri-bound was this intrepid crew.

"St. Jo" was the assembly point
Whence the wagon trains de-barked;
Each family unit was newly equipped
And prepared for departure in March.

What fortitude did men have then
Who trod the rigorous "Trail";
The torments were endured, as when
They set the "Schooners" sail.

The harsh winds screamed, the desert baked,
The "Prairie Schooners" rolled,
Each tortuous mile on mile ground by
So awfully, awfully slow.

Eight months it took to make the trip;
Edward was now fifty-nine;
His "Train" was number three to whip
The trail in "Forty-Five."

Late autumn found them near trail's end
Where flows the "Oregon,"
Still stood "Mazama's" peak to wend
Before their goal was won.

William was four as they crossed the plains,
Far too young to help the rest;
It seemed to him some pleasant game
As they struggled and wound their way west.

The "Train" then stopped, with trails-end gained
Near McLoughlin's "Vancouver" Fort;
Warm shelters thrown up to fend the rain
They gladly accepted the "Outpost's" support.

By Government "Act" in the year '49
Edward claimed a whole section of land;
The place that he chose was one of a kind,
Very rich, very wild, very grand.

His land was abreast the Columbia's shore,
On an emerald-green island it lay,
Few white men there had labour bore
Save its namesake, the Frenchman, Sauve.

The island was "Sauvies," as Edward lay claim
To his bountiful acres so new.
They lived from this land and its abundant wild game,
Their wants were simple and few.

Twelve children in all formed Ed's family plan
Each growing in their own special way;
Young William by now was becoming a man,
He would husband this land some day.

A man of the soil was serious young Bill,
Laboured long to establish his right;
Acquired the land, paid each share and fulfilled
All commitments to the family despite
Many obstacles he was destined to fight.

The test of a man to work hard and grow
In those desolate Pioneer days,
Makes us progeny warm in our feelings to know,
Our Sire Morgan had determined ways.

In spite of the harshness of Nature's rough hand,
Bill's family grew broad, made him proud;
Good provider was he on his bountiful land,
Stern heart, steadfast friend, all allowed.

He savored winter's wet grey dawn
Knew well the Honkers' call,
The willow hid the dappled fawn;
God's world seemed right for all.

Progress came to this harsh land
Where Chief Concomly roamed,
A short decade saw travel planned;
Steamboat whistles the Columbia toned.

The Eighties brought a grand new home
To William's burgeoning clan;
A mansion on a lush rich throne,
By whose shores the Columbia ran.

Great dinners were spread for friends that accrued,
For the Morgans were hosts at all times.
Gay days were enriched by Dame Sarah's firm view

That God's richest rewards are sublime.
She practiced his Word and teachings divine,
Making warmth for so many she knew.

The years have been kind to this historic band;
The Name, the Offspring, the Theme;
The Oldsters have passed to that far-away land,
The green-shuttered "Great House" too, is gone;
But memories are golden and the strain remains strong,
We descendants are grateful that we can belong
To the lineage of Edward, Mary, Sarah and Bill
Who planned so completely and bestowed us their will;
Their heritage for us to uphold and to guard,
Our family gift to sustain unmarred.

So, from our vantage view today
We heirs look back with pride,
Down through the corridor of years
Do note, strong principles applied.

Robert M. Morgan ~ 1971

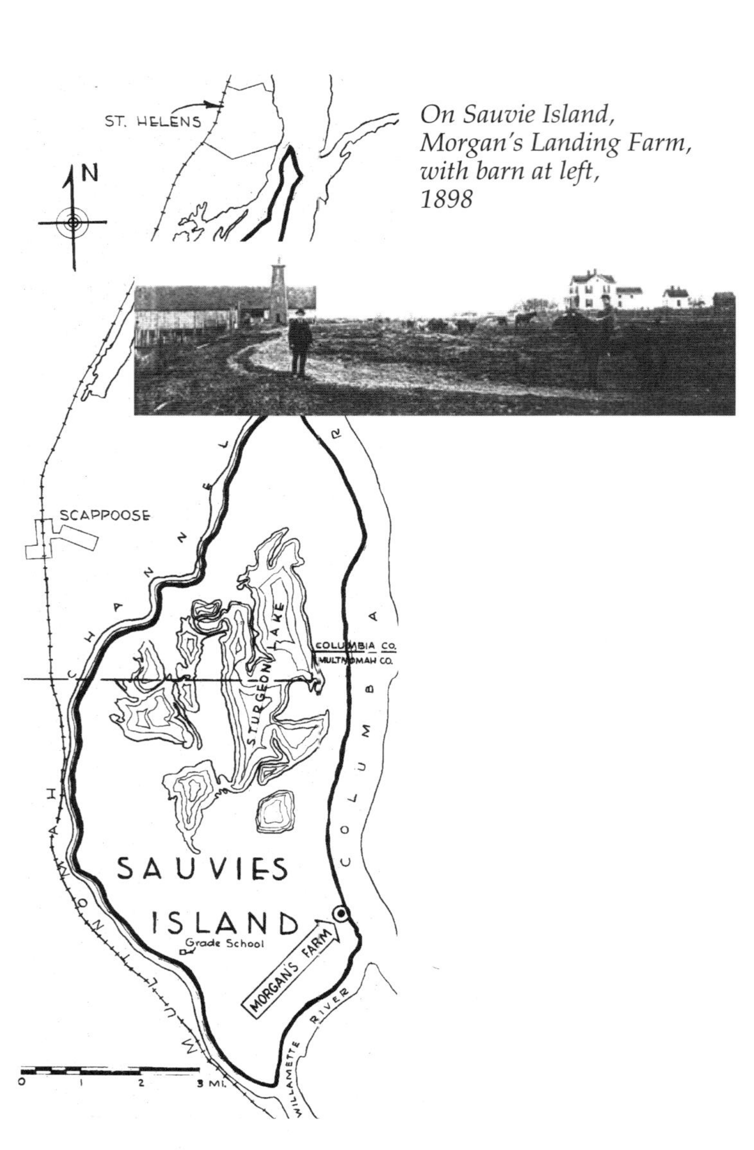

*On Sauvie Island,
Morgan's Landing Farm,
with barn at left,
1898*

PART ONE

THE EARLY YEARS

*T*he broad Columbia, Great River of The West, was calm and placid that late August morning. The warm summer sun made it shimmer and reflectively appear as a huge sheet of glass as its waters relentlessly sought their way toward the Pacific Ocean at a down stream current of four knots.

From upstream the agile little sternwheel steam work boat *Pronto*, property of the Port of Portland, upper-works gleaming with a fresh coat of white paint and big, newly re-finished sternwheel sparkling bright orange, made a 180-degree sweeping turn to port, cut her engines and came in quietly to briefly tie up at our big dock at Morgan's Landing Farm, home to the Morgan family for over 125 years.

Morgan's Landing, as such, was of special construction. Grandfather Morgan had built a huge barn, high above flood water, extending out about eighty feet from shore, with heavy substructure and decks at different levels to accommodate the daily river boats that served the family needs. The main structure, above the barn floor-level, housed a huge dairy-cow milking area with large hay storage. So expansive was this large structure, its imposing hulk standing as a sentinel, it was a river landmark to be seen for the entire length of that stretch of the Columbia.

Three large dolphins, each made up of five heavy wooden pilings standing upright and driven into the river bed in a group and tightly lashed together with several loops of one inch steel cable, served to protect the Landing as steam and diesel boats came in, variously, to tie up.

The *Pronto*, a 100-foot-long steam-driven sternwheeler of 400 horsepower, built in 1908 with plenty of muscle, was commissioned to tend the needs of the large suction-sand dredges owned by the Port of Portland for keeping the Willamette and Columbia River channels open adjacent to the cities of Portland, Oregon and Vancouver, Washington.

An open channel, forty feet deep and 500 feet wide all the way to the Pacific Ocean has made Portland one of the major Western seaports, principally for the export of lumber and grain.

Such actions as the docking of the little sternwheeler *Pronto*, and all other river activities too, did not go unnoticed by a nine-year-old boy, going on ten, that summer morning so long ago. I was the self-appointed sentinel that, among other things, watched the traffic with an ever discerning eye and ear. I knew most all of the steamboats that plied the rivers just by their distinctive whistles, night or day, even before they came into view.

The setting for our low-land 1000 acre farm certainly was near to being idyllic. The great white house, which faced east, sat nobly astride a man-made two acre knoll, high above the ravages of the annual spring floods, so common to the otherwise placid Columbia River.

Morgan Family Ranch Home
with green shutters and fancy balustrade

From the house veranda, fronting the river's western shore, a panorama of exceptional magnitude unfolded. The view there was unique in the river's entire course because its waters ran in a north-westerly direction before bending more to the west on their way to the Pacific ocean some 100 miles distant. Thirty-five miles east stood the Cascade Range with its bevy of mountains endlessly displaying their everlasting snows.

On clear days Mt. Rainier, far to the north, as one looked east, its 14,410 foot height commanded the horizon. Next was beautiful, ice-cream like, but troubled Mt.

St. Helens, lovely as she was before the days of the cataclysmic 1980 eruption tore her top away leaving a gaping crater to markedly mar her historic grace. Then the noble Mt. Adams stood just north of due east. Some 125 miles south of Mt. Adams was the jewel of all in the Cascades scene, Mt. Hood, 11,228 feet of snow-capped grandeur, a delight to all. Finally the precipitous tip of Mt. Jefferson, far to the south, made complete the back-drop for the setting of Morgan's Landing Farm that year of 1922 as the nation was readjusting from a deep recession following the end of World War I.

The Munro Sisters: Aunt Edna, Aunt Dorothy and Bessie Mae (left to right)

Bessie Mae Morgan (center) with friends

What were the family circumstances, graced by such a setting over seven decades ago? First though, something of my immediate parentage. I was the only living child of Newton Elmer Morgan and Bessie Mae Munro Morgan. I was born in a second floor flat near 18th and East Main Street in Portland, Oregon having been delivered by Doctor Bilderbach on March 3, 1913.

My dad, an even-tempered man of medium build, was somewhat unsettled most of his life, seemingly never quite satisfied. At age 17 he left the family farm that held so much for him, to go it on his own. By the time he was 20 years old, he had seen and done quite a lot. He sought attractions such as cowboying and mining, neither of which were the least bit rewarding. Returning to Portland to be with his parents Bill and Sarah, who by then had built a beautiful "city" home on East 22nd and Hawthorne Avenue, he cast about for new ventures.

Newton and Bessie Mae Morgan with infant Robert

By some good fortune he became acquainted with the George Munro family and soon thereafter his eye caught those of their next youngest daughter, Bessie Mae. Love at first sight barely describes their infatuation. They were married even though Newton still sought a secure means of livelihood.

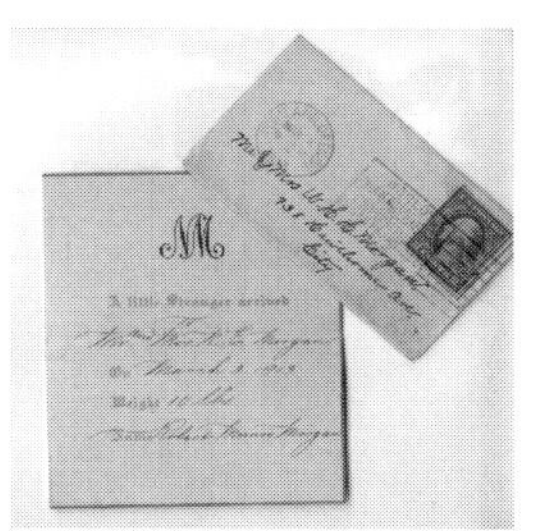

Birth Announcement, Robert M. Morgan

Bessie was a city girl. She and Newt had been married only a short while when Newton's wanderlust took them on a mining safari in the wilds of central eastern Nevada to the remote village of Pioche. Gratefully their tenure was limited. In later years, Mother would relate that they stayed in a rough, wood-sided mining shack and the pack-rats were so numerous she had to hang her shoes on the wall at night.

The five years following my parents' 1908 wedding, romantic as it must have been, were marred by the two miscarriages, certainly trying times for Mother prior to my arrival March 3, 1913.

By the time I was old enough to take notice of events at age three, Newt and Bessie, now with me included, were off again to a new life in The Dalles, Oregon where Dad took a mechanic's job.

Robert, age 3

Winters in The Dalles were often severe. My only recollection there was the snow piled high on each edge of the sidewalks as I rode my stuffed red cow on wheels.

The Dalles was an historic town by then almost 100 years old. It was the end of the torturous covered-wagon road, "The Oregon Trail." From the year 1843, the intrepid pioneers were obliged, at that point, to choose one of two routes into the Willamette Valley, the anticipated hinterland they had traveled so long to settle in.

One selection was to attempt passage on the inhospitable "Barlow Toll Road" carved through the Cascades mountains around the south side of Mt. Hood. So precipitous were some of the grades that the animals had to be unhitched and the covered wagons roped or winched up and down the barely discernable trail before re-hitching and proceeding on more acceptable terrain.

Equally ominous was the alternate choice of floating down the swift currents of the Columbia River as it raced through the ages-old gorge of the Cascade Mountains.

To prepare for that route required buying a ready-built raft or securing rough materials and building one of suitable dimensions and flotation to carry the covered wagon and all belongings.

The women, children, elders, oxen, horses and cattle followed downstream along a well marked Indian trail along the south river bank through the gorge to join up later with the men, who were tested to the utmost in negotiating the Columbia's fast waters.

The pioneers' decisions at The Dalles, always in the late fall following the travails of several months' transit from the starting point at St. Joseph, Missouri, tested the determinations of even the most stout-hearted.

Great Grandfather Edward Morgan, by then 57 years of age, Great Grandmother Mary, and family chose the Columbia river route. The family was made up of rugged sons of his first marriage and small children of their marriage, including my Grandfather William Henry Harrison, age five.

Great-Grandfather Edward Morgan, age 84

The sturdy family completed that final hazardous parcel of their 2000 mile trek west without losses, a most commendable feat. Many other pioneer families frequently lost loved ones as well as all belongings, attempting the challenges and rigors of the Columbia.

SARAH ELIZABETH ORCHARD MORGAN'S
CHINA DOLL

The family of Jesse and Minerva Medford Orchard had already traveled a great distance from their original home near Nacogdoches, Texas. After a year's sojourn in Illinois, they prepared to embark on their great adventure ~ the long Covered Wagon journey to a new life in the Oregon Territory.

An air of excitement surely must have gripped the Orchards and the others of their party as they made final preparations to take to the trail.

It was April, 1852; the last goodbyes had been said. Picture a little girl of four and one-half years, somewhat bewildered by all of the farewells. She was Sarah Elizabeth Orchard, born October 12, 1847, now bundled in the warmest clothes. She closely held her fondest possession, a lovely China doll. The time was at hand to climb aboard the great ox-drawn wagon, so carefully loaded with only the most necessary family belongings.

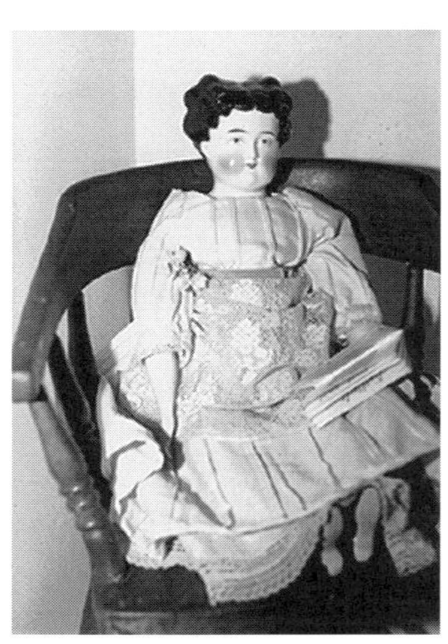

Sarah's China Doll

She held the doll with motherly instinct. At her tender age, she could not have foreseen that within a few short years, she would assume family responsibilities of her own, for she was to marry William Henry Harrison Morgan at the age of 17, on April 30, 1864. Sarah bore eleven chil-

dren, eight of whom grew to adulthood, expanding the Morgan Clan to ever greater numbers.

Sarah Elizabeth Orchard Morgan was a fine mother. As a small boy, I remember Grandmother Sarah as a sweet and gentle lady, so kind and mellow in her later years. A Godly woman. As I think of her now, her creed must have come from David's The Shepard Psalm ~ "Surely goodness and mercy shall follow me all the days of my life: and I will dwell in the house of the Lord forever."

Sarah's beautiful China doll became a family keepsake, somehow saved from the ravages of time, the raising of eight children and many moves from house to house as the family grew and changed dwellings on the Morgan donation land claim on Sauvie Island, Oregon.

By whatever decision, the China doll became the prized possession of Sarah's and William's daughter Daisy, who married Albert Demke and lived a happy life in Texas. After her death, the doll was kept by her son Donald Demke, who cherished its memories until his untimely death. Meanwhile, Albert remarried and he and his second wife Josephine lived many more happy years until his death. The lovely China doll, now diminished to only the head, shoulders and one arm, remained with its memories, passed along in the loving custody of Josephine Demke.

Although I had not known Josephine, by the most remarkable and providential circumstances, I was privileged to meet her at her comfortable home in Dayton, Texas, in late 1974. During that pleasant visit, "Aunt Jo" very graciously and with loving kindness gave me the doll. So now, even only partially complete, but including the original petticoat, Sarah's beautiful China doll again resided with one of her living grandsons.

Today, this lovely family heirloom reposes resplendent in the finest clothes, with refurbished body, yet still displaying that unusual antique lace bordered petticoat fashioned nearly a century and a half ago for little Sarah's pleasure.

Not being an ordinary doll, it would be expected that she be displayed in a most fitting way. Now she may be

*seen carefully placed in the "Little Pine High Chair," origi-
nally purchased by Mother Sarah Morgan for her youngest son, Newton Elmer Morgan. The highchair, however,
served many of the young descendants of Sarah and William, and is still used regularly in our home to elevate and
comfortably feed the newest generation of Morgans as they
come into this world and take their place in the family
scheme.*

*We cherish the legend of Sarah's lovely China doll which
so appropriately exemplifies the substance and foundation
of our grand American way of life. We trust the new and
coming generations will attach some of the same sentiment
to these things that hold us to a great family heritage.*

Robert M. Morgan ~ 1986

When Dad and Mother decided to leave The Dalles
and return to Portland, the trip became one of my most
memorable and exciting adventures. It was the opening
chapter for my childhood-based attraction to steam boating.

Daily river boat service between The Dalles and Portland was a public pleasure in 1917, not new, however, having been an important part of the intermediate river system since the completion of the Cascade Locks and canal
in the last decade of the Nineteenth Century.

That year Dad had bought tickets for us and our sparse
baggage aboard the fine sternwheel steamboat *Dalles City*,
a fast, commodious packet, built in 1898. She was 152 feet
long, with a 30.9 foot beam, 8.2 foot depth of hold and
powered by port and starboard 16 inch bore X 72 inch
stroke steam engines connected to huge arms, in turn attached to the cranks which turned the massive sternwheel
to create a very acceptable water surface speed of 14 knots.

The *Dalles City* galley, located amidships on the main
deck, astern of the boiler room and forward of the engine

room, served up the fine meals which were elevated to the second deck dining salon. The galley's chef was a most gracious Chinese cook.

As a four-year-old, my most memorable experience on that exciting trip downriver was receiving a freshly baked piece of chocolate cake direct from the smiling chef.

Sternwheelers like the Dalles City *were the most reliable way to travel before highways were dependable and railroads served the region.*

SKIMMED MILK AND GRAIN TAILINGS

The growing-up experiences, many of which I have touched on elsewhere in this running story remain, as should be expected, in my mature yet aging mind.

Camping, hunting, fishing, and going to the Weatherly Ice Cream Plant, are but a few of those memories so securely tucked away, sometimes surfacing to picture a distant happening.

Mother used to take me to the farm for a few days during the years that Uncle Win and Aunt Luella and my cousins lived in the great white house.

Elsewhere mentioned was the hog house on Grandfather's ranch. At some point in the ranch history, Uncle Win and Grandfather must have concluded that they should try raising hogs and thereby taking advantage of "swill/whey" as hog feed, which accumulated from the skim milk generated in the dairy as milk was separated from the cream which then went to market. The cream separator discharged the skim milk into large 50-gallon wooden barrels which stood waiting on a huge horse-drawn wooden sled. About three times weekly, Uncle Win hauled the sled load of whey to the hog house, about a quarter-mile away. In warm weather, the skim milk quickly turned to noxious whey as it stood in the huge barrels which were never washed. Whey, when mixed with grain tailings, made a good feed for the hogs.

On the trips to the hoghouse, Uncle Win would hook "Trilby," a huge grey mare, to the sled-barrel combination and take off, slopping some of the whey as the sled was dragged over the uneven farm road. There was room behind the second barrel for me to ride as I hung to the mouth or edge of the rear barrel. This to me at age 5 was a not-to-be missed adventure, messy and smelly as it distinctly was.

THE BASKET SOCIAL

Affable Uncle Win was not really a farmer at heart. Regaled in braided uniform and cap, he was more comfortably a steamboat Captain, as he appeared on that lovely day when he met cute Luella Morgan, youngest daughter of the clan. Her winsome ways soon overcame Winfred Copeland. He straightway gave up his budding captain's career, married Luella, agreeing to move to the farm so that they, in marital bliss, could be together in a farm atmosphere. Upon moving to the farm, former Captain Copeland had much to learn about day-to-day farming. He was obliged to sort of patch his way along as he performed the many tasks of farming.

My Dad Newton was a mechanic. As a farmer, he was quite efficient at keeping machinery and other farm gear in good order. Newt the handyman lacked several of the fine personal attributes of his brother-in-law Winfred. Often times he was critical of Uncle Win's rather "hay wire" way of keeping such gear as horse's harnesses patched together.

Elsewhere in this running story, I touched on the community's pie and basket socials and school parties, always immensely enjoyed, particularly by us kids, but always occurring too infrequently. Those affairs were always held at the huge, neighboring Gillihan ranch house, some two miles distance from the Morgan ranch house.

One stormy winter Western Oregon night, Dad, Mother and I joined Uncle Win and family to travel to Gillihan's ranch in Uncle Win's two-seated buggy drawn by Uncle's mismatched two-horse team, bedecked in a badly worn harness he had hurriedly wired and tied together with scraps of fish-net cotton cord and haywire.

That night, the winds and rain were relentless. Well bundled against the elements, we arrived at Gillihan's for a grand evening. The highlight was a "Basket Social." Each basket, of the tenderest of morsels, including cake or pie prepared by the ladies, was auctioned off to the highest bidder. Maximum bid allowed was $1.50. I always tried for Hilda Lerch's basket; sometimes Cousin Jim Copeland outbid me. Proceeds went for supplies for the one-room Gillihan district #11 school.

The storm increased during the evening. Returning home, the heavily loaded buggy with eight of us aboard, including cousin Scott who was just a baby in arms, groaned as the horses dragged it through the increasingly sticky mud. Suddenly, at the worst possible point, the horses lurched as they pulled. The buggy stuck and the harness broke as the rain fell in torrents.

There we were, in the dead of night, bogged down in Gillihan's woods. The men had not thought of bringing a lantern and were obliged to grope in the dark and somehow patch the soggy harness together. We nine year-olds, Jim and I, pushed with the men as the horses errantly strained, finally pulling the buggy free from the mire. We boys walked the rest of the distance home, as did Newt, who was not the least bit hesitant in objecting to the flimsy state of the harness gear. All the while, though silently, Uncle Win drove the buggy and praised the Lord for deliverance from a trying situation.

Back in the big city of Portland, our family of three soon located in the nice rented brown house at 721 E. Main Street, only three blocks east of the flat where I had been born. That quiet neighborhood became packed

Our rented brown house on 421 East Main Street

with lasting memories amid my childish dreams.

My Grandparents, W. H. H. and Sarah Elizabeth's fine "city" home located at 22nd and East Hawthorne, an important east-west thoroughfare, was just three short blocks from our East Main Avenue brown house. My grandparents' beautiful stately home, three stories high above a full basement, sat astride an ample corner lot facing Hawthorne Avenue. The house had a wide veranda skirting the north and east sides. The great front door opened into an inviting entrance hall. Straight ahead was a fine, open stairway leading upstairs. The third-floor completely finished attic was a treasure-trove of family things for me to examine on my frequent visits

William Henry Harrison Morgan and Sarah Elizabeth Orchard Morgan, courtesy of June Tillman

to Grandmother's house. Outside, adjacent to the manicured grounds, Grandfather had included a fine two-car garage, unusual for that day. But, when they first moved into the house, Grandfather bought a

Grandparents' ornate entrance hall on East Hawthorne

new car, took driving lessons, and promptly had a serious accident involving, I believe, a fatality. He abruptly sold the car, never attempting to drive again. For years the garage stood empty, equipped with a never used private gasoline tank and pump. The accident and Grandfather's reluctance to drive again were things the family never talked about.

The final days and months of World War I wore away. Mother's older sister, Aunt Edna, an army nurse, was temporarily living with us during those momentous days. It was quite common for her to graciously invite newly hospital-released returning war veterans to our brown house for a delicious home-cooked meal. I was fascinated with those servicemen and their uniforms and hard earned decorations.

Armistice Day came in late 1918. Mother took me over to Hawthorne Avenue to watch and wave to the returning troops in the seemingly huge victory parade. Leading the celebration of marching men, colors and bands was a glowing President Woodrow Wilson, triumphantly occupying the rear seat of an elegant, black Winton touring car with its top down. Presidents publicly appeared then in ways unthinkable now.

By the end of War I, Dad had been a mechanic for Fred Dundee in his East Water Street garage enough to become known in the trade and was soon led to a good job working on model T light-delivery trucks in the large shop of the Weatherly Ice Cream Company. The plant was located on Grand Avenue and East Alder Street in Portland. George Weatherly became one of Dad's good friends.

My father, Newton Elmer Morgan

My father's tools, including a model T Ford spark plug wrench, a plate glass cutting tool, T valve feeler gauge and T valve grinding tool.

As a boy of 6, a highlight in my many memories was a visit with Dad to the Weatherly truck shop. Dad worked on the little brightly painted model T panel deliveries. I keep a display of some of the "T" tools he used with dexterity as a young man. More spectacular than the model Ts, for me, were the huge three and five ton Garford and Vehlie, hard rubber-tired trucks used to haul ice, salt and ice cream making equipment.

A trip to the shop was always highlighted with a visit to the ice cream factory freezers with their ever-present strong ammonia smell, for a tempting serving of delicious Weatherly Ice Cream.

Something again happened with Dad's work, causing still another change, and we moved to Pendleton, Oregon. Pendleton, in the heart of Eastern Oregon's rolling wheat growing plateaus and hills, was to me, by then age 6, just another extension of life's wonderment and exciting new things to do.

Dad soon found a small house to rent on the southeast edge of town on a gravel road. Across from us was a farm-house and our only neighbors. Our house, if nothing more, was some improvement for Mother to get out of the dingy flat on the Umatilla River that we occupied briefly. I believe the house was rented to us furnished, which as I recall was something of an over-statement. Mother made a bed for me on a sort of sofa in the living room. The first night, after the lights were out, I learned of something new, bed-bugs. The next day, Mother somehow got rid of them.

Many good and memorable things happened as the folks made a new home in that pleasant community. Dad's wages must have been favorable. It wasn't long until he bought a used 1915 4-cylinder Chevrolet touring car that took us many places. Soon thereafter, a most important event happened. Dad and Mother went shopping and brought home, on trial, a music machine, an Edison turn table with records a quarter inch thick that produced the most beautiful music. Although the Edison was good sounding, they decided to try another and finally settled on a Mandell record player contained in a conventional tall cabinet on legs with casters. To play records, its hinged top opened. Although the Mandell didn't survive in competition as did the Victrola, it gave us entertainment for many years and I thought it was wonderful.

We didn't stay long in the little rented house on the edge of Pendleton as spring approached. During the months there, however, Dad and Mother noticed something a bit extraordinary about the farmstead and house of our neighbors across the gravel road. On certain evenings, there were often many cars parked out near the barn. Dad, having become acquainted, found that the attraction was illegal gamecock fighting, a grisly pastime that he showed me one night much to Mother's consternation and objections.

Becoming more acquainted in town, Dad met Mr. Foster, a wealthy wheat rancher who was willing to rent his commodious home across town. It was in the best neighborhood in Pendleton where we lived for the duration of our stay in Eastern Oregon. My Aunt Edna again came to live with us, spending the summer months. It was a good period. Mother had a very comfortable house to keep, and she had the company of her sister. We had many weekend trips into the country in the little, slightly decrepit Chevy. Dad took me on my first trout fishing outing. We caught our limit. Dad was a hunter and we spent many hours out in the prairies hunting jack-rabbits with his 22 automatic rifle. One time when Mother was along, Dad shot a jack-rabbit, and I ran to retrieve it. Carrying it back in one hand, Mother was appalled to find my arm black with fleas.

That summer when Aunt Edna was with us, she by some means became acquainted with Mr. Ransom. I thought he was great. A weekend camping trip was planned to Lehman Hot Springs in the Blue Mountains.

It was primitive camping, but an idyllic spot. Lots of wild animals, always a delight to me, and excellent trout fishing were part of my great recollections that final year in Eastern Oregon.

Some time before, Mother had arranged for me to be baptized by sprinkling in the Methodist Church. Her folks, my maternal grandparents George and Mae Munro, had been members of that faith in Grand Ledge, Michigan. Aunt Edna, Mother and Uncle George, Jr., my most favorite uncle, were born there. The Munro family had migrated to Portland, Oregon about 1900. Their youngest child, Aunt Dorothy, was born in Portland in 1903. My incomprehensible loss early on, was that Grandfather George and Grandmother Mae both departed from this earth before I was old enough to know them.

The family times were precious. Grandmother Mae Munro's sister, Great Aunt Nora, had preceded the others to Oregon and had married a young druggist, John Laue, who became a renowned pharmacist. His main store was located at Third and Yamhill in downtown Portland. It was a place where I spent much time as I was growing up. His second drug store was at 22nd and West Burnside.

Among my most fond memories were the dual celebrations of Uncle John's and my birthdays, mine the third and his the fourth of March. Uncle John, a five foot five inch jolly Dutchman, always requested his favorite banana cream cake as topping for that gathering, a decision that fit my palate exactly.

Great Aunt Ella lived in a rural setting near the end of the St. Johns electric streetcar line. That was about an hour and a half ride and two transfers away from where we boarded the Hawthorne Avenue street car on East 20th near the brown house. To me it was worth every minute of what to Mother must have been a somewhat tiring ride. Near the point of debarkation, she would signal the motorman to stop in the middle of a pasture. We would get off the street car and walk a dirt path about a quarter mile to Aunt Ella's house. On a hot summer day, there was always a cool refreshing drink for us. Automatic electric residential refrigeration was still a long way off.

Grandmother Mae's maiden name was Taply. I was

never sure as to her brothers and sisters. But Great Aunts Nora, Ella and Effie had by some means settled in the Portland area prior to the turn of the century. I was reminded of the Taply family whenever I heard Mother singing the grand old gospel hymn, *Love Lifted Me*. The beginning words of the first verse, which I have known since age 4, are:

> *I was sinking deep in sin,*
> *Far from the peaceful shore.*
> *Very deeply stained within,*
> *Sinking to rise no more.*
> *But the Master of the sea*
> *Heard my despairing cry.*
> *From the waters, he lifted me;*
> *Now safe am I.*

It was 1921 and a whole different world was soon to unfold for me as Dad finally came to the point of removing himself from being an auto mechanic. He chose, with Grandfather Morgan's persuasion, to return to the place of Dad's birth, Morgan's Landing Farm on Sauvie Island. Although Mother used to take me to visit the farm when Uncle Win and Aunt Louella Copeland lived there, it was soon going to be our immediate family home. My memories of the warm atmosphere of Aunt Lou's home and its kitchen fragrances were unforgettable, too.

THE GROCERY BOAT

Magnificent as the great White house on the Morgan ranch was prior to 1925, isolation held it apart from the rest of the world. No roads, telephones or electricity or stores made the city of Portland, a bare 14 miles distance to the south, almost as far away as if it were three counties distant. Living on Sauvie Island cultivated self-sufficiency amongst the Islanders.

Although not a consistent service on our section of the lower Columbia River, the "Grocery Boat," placed in operation primarily to serve the commercial fishermen and isolated river people, was a unique and most welcome attraction on those occasional times it tied up at Morgan's Landing Farm. The first time the boat stopped at our dock, I immediately boarded it, marveling at the wondrous, though limited assortment of candies, cookies and staple grocery items.

After a detailed inspection of so many desirables, I raced ashore and back up to the house. There I implored Mother to come at once to see the treasure of things to eat that were tied up at our landing. To my disappointment, she flatly said no for two reasons. First, she was afraid of the water and would not attempt, under any circumstances, to walk the narrow gang-plank to board the boat. Secondly, she advised that the prices would be way too high and she had no money to spend for candy or cookies. What I had thought would bring about some toothsome fancies frittered away and my enthusiasm for the "Grocery Boat" waned.

Morgan's Landing Farm, so much a part of my early life, was no more than lush green bottom land, interspersed with mirror lakes and nature's intermittent plantings of oak, willow, ash and cottonwood trees when Great-Grandfather Edward Morgan and family first viewed it as a potential land to live on that day in 1846.

The United States government was soon to make Oregon Territory land of choice available to pioneers such as the Morgans by enactment of the Donation Land Act allotting a section, one square mile, of land to a man and wife that would agree to live on it. That certain 640 acres Edward and Mary Shirley Morgan chose was filed for in February 1849 under the terms of the "act." It proved to be a prolific, bountiful land for the Morgan clan.

William Henry Harrison Morgan, my Grandfather, but 5 years old in 1845 when the family crossed the plains, grew to manhood. When his father Edward died, he formed a plan to purchase the family land from the other heirs, his brother and sisters. Paying each heir in gold coin, he proceeded to increase his property until he owned 1000 acres and eventually built the great white house that would become my home.

By the time Dad, Mother and I moved to the farm in 1921, it was a fine farming enterprise consisting of the green-shuttered white house, several small out-buildings, a fine horse barn, the big dock barn of Morgan's Landing and three other large cattle barns and a newly built hog house. Cattle feeding and dairying were the main farm enterprises.

The beautifully located property, with its comfortable facilities was so near, 12 miles, and yet so far from the big city of Portland, we were in effect isolated on Sauvie Island. The Burlington Ferry to the mainland, on the back south side of the Island, was 7 miles from our beautiful east side fronting the Columbia River. Paved roads extended only part way, the remaining distance to the farm were ruts through fields and prairies with seven gates to open and close in transit.

The island farms were so far apart, neither electric power nor telephone service came to our side until 1935. Domestic water was always a problem along the river as the shoreline subterranean strata contained no gravel formation. Shallow surface wells were rarely acceptable. We used river water for washing and bathing.

The creamery in Portland where Dad shipped the dairy milk always steam-cleaned the 10 gallon cans when emptied. Then one was filled with fine Portland Bull-Run water for our domestic use. The daily steamer *America*, an

America steam-propeller, freight and passenger boat, seen here loading 10-gallon milk cans, Multnomah Channel, Sauvie Island, circa 1910. Later rebuilt with full second deck cabins for Ladies and Men.

agile propeller-boat about 85 feet long with full cabins on deck two and a pilot house atop the third deck. It stopped daily at Morgan's Landing Farm at 9:00 a.m. to load the milk cans on its way to Portland. Promptly at 4:00 p.m. that afternoon, it returned, off-loading the empties and our drinking water.

BIB OVERALLS and UNITED AIRLINES

Barely more than a toddler, I first viewed commercial passenger airplanes landing and taking off from Portland, Oregon's municipal Swan Island airfield along the

Willamette River. Only five years old at the time, I stood with my family on the bluffs above Mocks Bottom, near the St. Johns District. We watched as acrobatic stunt planes maneuvered high above the primitive airstrip. I couldn't have imagined that within a few short years, I would be flying hundreds of business hours on pioneer aircraft that displayed the signature colors of United Airlines. In the meantime, another aviation adventure would add to my attraction to air travel.

On a cold, fog-shrouded winter afternoon, as a thirteen-year-old on Morgan's Landing Farm, my attention was suddenly drawn to the drone of a large airplane engine directly overhead. Listening intently, I caught changes in the aircraft engine's rhythm. It abruptly stopped a seemingly short distance away. I rushed a few hundred yards to an open pasture in the direction from which the engine sounds were last heard. To my amazement, I could see the dim outline of the hulk of a large airplane taxiing over the rough terrain toward me. I would soon learn that it was a Boeing early model 80A bi-plane distinctly bearing the trademark colors of United Airlines.

The pilot, attempting to land at Swan Island field, found Portland socked in. On a second fly-over, however, he saw a "hole" in the fog, dropped down through it and landed unceremoniously on Morgan's Landing Farm acreage. As he shoved open the cabin door, fortunately sans any passengers, his eye caught sight of an overalls-clad boy scurrying toward the plane. With a worried-sounding, clipped introduction, he succinctly explained his predicament, saying that he must hasten to deliver his valuable cargo of registered United States Mail to Swan Island field, first making a phone call to identify his emergency location.

Just as abruptly, as teenagers are prone to converse, I told him that we didn't have phone service. Then he asked if our family had a car. I responded that we did have a nice Buick, but that Dad had milking and other dairy work to do. Proudly, I explained that I could drive, but was only thirteen and had no driver's license. The pilot then commanded me to run to the house, explain the urgency, and arrange some quick transportation while he stood by the plane, guarding it and its precious cargo.

Mother Bessie Morgan was overwhelmed by such short-notice excitement and the exacting turn of events. Dad Newt Morgan, realizing the urgency, concluded that I could reliably take the car, with Bessie riding along as counselor and chaperone. Rushed, she gathered her coat and hand-bag. Quickly getting in the Buick, we crossed the fields to the airplane where the pilot, with a 45-Colt strapped at his side, bruskly loaded the mailbags and himself into the back seat.

The only route to the county road was through several farm gates which I was obliged to open, drive through, stop, and close each one and then proceed as fast as possible. Finally on the county gravel road, we soon arrived at the Burlington Ferry, crossed the Multnomah Channel, then drove up and onto Highway 30 into St. Johns, and down to Swan Island airfield. With an air of great authority, the pilot grabbed the mail bags and disembarked the car. He then handed Bessie a $20.00 bill, and with a terse "thank you," he quickly disappeared into a nearby hanger.

Still flushed with the fervor of that unusual afternoon of events, Mother and I drove back to our farm. The next morning, the sun broke through bright and clear. Shortly, three United Airlines vehicles arrived. After carefully checking the pasture terrain and expertly warming the engine of the beautiful Boeing aircraft, a test pilot taxied out for maximum clear-

Gillihan School House,
courtesy June Tillman

ance. With a perfect take-off, the striking plane flew off into the bright blue winter sky.

This complete affair was the opening chapter of my life-long attraction to United Airlines and the graceful aircraft I would later learn to know so well.

Frigid January winters, when the sub-freezing east winds blew down the Columbia Gorge and across the Island flatlands, our water pump suction pipe always froze.

Farm life on Sauvie Island, though isolated, was interlaced with the ever-present river traffic. Everything was so different from the town and city ways. It was an early chapter of the myriad new things I had to learn and do.

The District 11 Gillihan one-room school, housing all eight grades, was where I enrolled for the 3rd grade that fall. It was a challenging experience and a two-mile walk from our ranch house. With no running water, electricity or telephone, it was distinctively different with a pot-bellied wood-burning stove in the center of the schoolroom, plus a common-use drinking water pail that the teacher carried three quarters of a mile each day to and from the Gillihan home where she boarded. The heavy pungent scent of the oiled floor lingers in my senses. The outdoor privies for boys and girls were primitive attachments to the scene, too. My first year there, a hemp rope swing tied to a cottonwood branch was the only play equipment.

Learning to apply oneself in a room where someone was almost always talking was a concentration challenge to me. School plays and a couple of pie or basket socials, always held at the large Gillihan ranch house, were highlights that remain well tucked away in my memories.

THE "REAL BOAT BOY"

Eight-year-old boys have glorious dreams; they imagine themselves as many things. He grew up on the shores of "The Great River Of The West," Oregon's Columbia River. The river action was made lively by many beautiful big shining white sternwheel steamboats, so named because a very large paddle wheel powered with a steam engine propelled them through the water.

*In his imagination, being the "Real Boat Boy" was something different than just being a rowboat with oars, and certainly **not** a little canoe and paddle.*

There was a sense of something grand in thinking he was a massive sternwheel steamboat, three decks high. He chose a name from the dozens of steamboats he knew so well that were on the river. No Wonder had a freshly painted, orange colored stern paddle wheel.

Many sternwheelers and surely the No Wonder were work boats built with a towing mast located just behind the tall smoke stack that belched great puffs of mixed white steam and smoke. From the river banks, the sounds of her exhaust steam and smoke sounded like "WHOO-USH, WHOO-USH" as the No Wonder struggled upstream against the river current pulling a long log raft of beautiful fir or hemlock saw logs.

There were few store-bought toys for country lads of eight such as this "Real Boat Boy" whose farm life was years before electric lights, television, telephones and alas, an ice cream delivery man. But he didn't mind, his "make-believe" was easy for him to fashion his way of playing. He became a sternwheel steamboat himself.

In the soft river beach sand which to him was make-believe water, he would pull three or four eight-foot bean poles, tied together as a raft of logs. Using his feet as a make-believe paddle wheel, he would kick up waves of dry sand which, to him, appeared like the huge sternwheel *churning rolling waves of water behind it. He would imagine, for hours, that he was the sternwheeler <u>No Wonder</u> moving along, ever so slowly, pulling his make-believe log raft.*

His body was the imaginary main part of the steamboat. His head however, was the "Pilot House," with glass windows on all sides, so the "Captain," dressed in his elegant, gold braid-trimmed uniform and cap, could see in all directions as he steered the <u>No Wonder</u> with the big wooden steering wheel. When signaling the other boats, the Captain would pull the cord attached from the ceiling that blew the triple-toned steam whistle mounted on the big smokestack.

The "Real Boat Boy" play-worked for hours at <u>No Wonder's</u> toiling towing. He didn't mind if Grown-Ups saw him imitating a steamboat, but he preferred to go about his play-task, undisturbed and unidentified.

Now, many years later, the great sternwheel steamboats are gone from the mighty Columbia River, the boy long-since has become a man who still treasures the times that passed all too fast in his dream-filled childhood.

<u>No Wonder</u> was originally built in 1877 at Portland, Oregon by Mr. Weidler whose family name remains of historic importance in that city. He cut lumber and seasoned it for two years before constructing his sternwheel steamboat which he named <u>Wonder</u>. Everybody wondered where he got the money to build such boat, and why? But after being built, it did such a good job towing logs that they all agreed, "No wonder he built it." Rebuilding it years later in 1889, he was pleased to re-name his creation <u>No Wonder.</u>

Back at the farm, my after-school chores of filling the kitchen and living room woodboxes were promptly executed as I savored the elegant smells emanating from kettles and the stove oven as mother prepared the always flavorful ranch suppers.

By the time I was ten years old, I got up with Dad at 5:30 each morning and milked 6 cows by hand before breakfast. Then I walked to school. By age 14, I was milking half of our 45-cow dairy herd with the new Pine Tree-Surge milking machine Dad had just installed. By age 16, twenty-year-old Lyle Lipp, our hired man and I were milking 60 cows night and morning. Lyle, a good worker did the chores and mid-day farm work. By then I had started to Scappoose High School, which involved driving my well-used 1924 model T Ford roadster to Burlington, across the ferry on the mainland, to catch the school bus for the 12 mile ride to school.

MY MODEL T FORD BUG

As we approach mid-way through the last decade of the twentieth century, few today have the faintest notion as to what a "Bug" is or was.

My Dad was still a comparatively young man when I was thirteen approaching fourteen. By then a dairy farmer, he was also a very "handy man" with tools, probably due to his earlier training as a model T Ford mechanic.

Dad concluded I must have transportation when I started my first year of high school since we lived seven miles from Highway 30 where the Scappoose school bus would pick me up. He arranged to build me a "Bug" (a little car) from gathered parts. Contacting his old friend and former employer, George Weatherly, of Weatherly Ice Cream Company, he bought one of their abandoned Ford chassis, formerly a delivery rig.

Such a chassis consisted of a frame, springs, front and rear axles, engine/transmission, steering-wheel, radiator and four wheels with tires. On the bare frame, with his carpentry-skills, he fashioned a wooden body consisting only of a driver's seat forward of a small luggage box.

With no fenders, lights or top, the "Bug" was the barest sort of vehicle. Such a stripped unit was not licensable.

I could, however, drive it cross-country to the Burlington Ferry landing. Dad had arranged with his cousin-by-marriage, Hugh Graham, for me to park the "Bug" in Hugh's grove of fir trees adjacent to the ferry landing. I could then cross on the ferry and walk half a mile to the Burlington store to catch the school bus.

Such a detailed travel route was fine in the open-air "Bug" until the Oregon fall rains began. As the rains came, something more storm-resistant was soon necessary and I reluctantly abandoned the "Bug" for school travel when, for $200.00, Dad bought me a used 1924 model T Ford roadster, with side curtains.

The "Bug," although not adequately functional for winter travel, was an open-air fun rig which I had great times with in the open fields that fourteenth year of my simple farm life before advancing to the enclosed comfort of the T roadster.

My completely restored duplicate of the original Model A Ford Roadster

The year 1929 was an eventful year. My old model T for which Dad had paid $200.00, had served faithfully through my sophomore and junior years. However, the muddy, barely discernable, rutted roads had taken their toll. The winter of 1928-29, I wore out four sets of tire chains. When summer came, as I anticipated my high school senior year in the fall, Dad and I concluded I needed a better car. That conclusion was electric. He traded the model T for a sparkling new, rose-beige model A Ford deluxe roadster with rumble seat. The delivered list price was $675.00. I don't recall the trade-in allowance on the model T. Our agreement was that I would work on the farm for $35.00 a month and make payments on the new model A of $30.00 per month. Dad paid for the insurance and I could use the farm gasoline which cost Dad 11 cents per gallon, delivered by boat in 50-gallon drums.

That year, the Multnomah County Road Department surveyed and acquired right-of-way easements for a much needed road. The road right-of-way through the Morgan ranch was about 3/4 mile long. Dad applied for and received a contract for the light earthmoving required to bring the road base to grade. Dad provided the 2-horse team and Fresno scraper and I became the driver on that contract job moving dirt. I learned a lot about moving dirt with a team, pulling a Fresno scraper, and earned the handsome sum of $3.00 per hour for the portion of the project that ran through the Morgan property. I fast became a muscular man.

My senior high year was great. My grades were average. I was first string left guard on the Scappoose Warriors varsity football team. I went to my first dances at Florence Auto Park hall near Scappoose. Sometime that fall, the slick new model A Ford roadster helped me get my first date.

The winter of 1929-30 was one of the most severe in many years. Lyle and I were milking about 60 cows. Dad was showing signs of tiring of farming and had evidenced strong interest in selling Surge milking machines. Following Christmas, he left Mother, Lyle and me with the dairy to run and went on a sales trip to Stockton, California.

The weather turned cold on January 5th. The Columbia river became choked with ice which built up huge cakes along the shoreline as the tide ebbed and flowed. All wooden hulled river boats stopped running, including the steamer *America* that served us. The more placid Willamette River and the Multnomah channel that skirted the mainland side of Sauvie Island froze solid with six to eight inches of clear ice.

Lyle and I and our 60 cows were challenged in the subfreezing temperatures. All water pipes were frozen. Moisture that accumulated in the milking machine vacuum lines froze, forcing us to milk by hand. With no boat service, the *whole milk* built up at a rate of about 120 gallons per day. The milk soon filled all of the empty 10-gallon cans, all of which promptly froze. Our only option was to rig up the old cream separator, thaw each frozen can of *whole milk* and separate the cream.

Confronted with those alarming conditions, besides the milking routine, it took us two days to separate the cream from all of the surplus milk. Furthermore, with no running water, we had to break mounds of built-up river ice twice a day so the animals could get drinking water.

On the third day of this rigorous routine, I loaded 5-gallon cans of cream in the model A and drove across the island to where the Burlington Ferry was frozen in 8 inches of solid ice. There was plenty of action at that point because all of the dairymen on the island, suffering the same problems we had, were carrying their milk or cream across the ice to waiting trucks on the mainland side. I carried our cream across the ice, too.

Dad returned to the island about January 15th as the frigid weather subsided to find everything on the ranch returned to normal. It took me several hours to relate my teen-age experiences to him. This was yet another phase in my growing-up, supported as always, by Mother's superb homemaking.

UNCLE GEORGE

My Uncle George Munro was a robust, genial man who had served the public most of his life as an over-the-road bus driver. He was married first to Janie, a cute lady who bore him a daughter, my cousin Jean. Whatever the reasons, a divorce caused my cousin to be bounced around far too much as a young girl. Although she spent some time living with us, in my Mother's care, life was not easy for her.

Several years after Uncle George's divorce from Janie, he became more successful in the bus business. It was some time in those gathering years that he met and soon married Eve Woodruff, an equally lovely lady that all the family liked.

As mentioned before, we had few gravel roads, and least of all paved roads, on the Island in 1924. That Thanksgiving, my folks had invited Uncle George and Aunt Eve and one of her sisters to come to the farm to stay overnight before the Thanksgiving festivities. Dad had suggested to Uncle George to start early because of the practically nonexistent road the last three miles to the house.

It was a typically wet, stormy November afternoon when the Munros were to arrive. Mother had made elaborate preparations for the folks' stay. As an eleven-year-old, I looked forward with great anticipation to my favorite Uncle's arrival with his recent bride and new sister-in-law. Uncle could hold my attention endlessly as he spun story after tale about his experiences on the highways of the West and the wonderful White and Pierce-Arrow buses he drove with such dexterity.

About five o'clock that stormy late afternoon with darkness approaching, I took up my common post in the loft over the woodshed in the great white house where I had a commanding view out across the ranch bottom lands. It was there the rutted road led across the last mile to our ranch house and buildings, on higher ground.

Shortly after five, sure enough, I saw headlights in the distance which I knew to be those of Uncle George's fine seven-passenger Cadillac touring car, snugly fitted with side curtains and hot air heater. The headlights seemed to be approaching quite normally until they came upon the area Dad and I knew to be the muddiest and slickest, particularly when the rain came down in sheets as it was that evening. Soon, the headlights stopped. I knew at once that Uncle George was stuck. I scrambled down from the loft, got into my boots and slicker, and told Mother the folks were near, but stuck. Then I ran the half mile to where they were, having grabbed up an armful of gunny sacks to put under the tires for traction.

After greeting Uncle and the women, I laid out the sacks in front of the rear tires. With me pushing, Uncle was able to move the car forward past the sacks, only to again become stuck in the slippery mud. We repeated laying the sacks out for traction, this time Uncle George said to me, "You drive, and I'll push." Starting easily in low gear, at a slow engine speed, the big car crept along to higher ground where I stopped.

That opportunity was like heaven to me, just to be sitting behind the wheel of that magnificent automobile and applying power in a progressive way. On more firm ground, Uncle jumped on the running board, with me driving and the women applauding. We soon reached sandy soil and good traction. Both Uncle and the woman were full of praise for my help in bringing them through the mud.

Once in the house, I received all sorts of praise. To say the least, the experience of driving the Cadillac, at even two or three miles per hour, was an exhilarating thrill. That was a memory, tucked away for all time about my Uncle George who was a sort of champion by my standards.

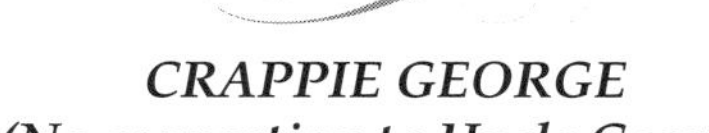

CRAPPIE GEORGE
(No connection to Uncle George)

Crappie, a genus of small North American Sunfish, is found in sluggish streams and ponds. Webster and I each knew of Crappies. In my intense, chock-full early years, I fished by the hour for the succulent one-pound to two-pound Crappie, which I brought to the Great Ranch house. Mother reluctantly cooked them for me.

He was a generally silent, somewhat mysterious character, Crappie George. None of us Islanders ever knew his full name. Dad reckoned that he probably lived in a Portland "skid-row" flophouse. To me, however, he was something much more, an intriguing somebody who unceremoniously occasionally stepped from the decks of the Steamer America as it made its afternoon stop at Morgan's Landing Farm.

No ordinary figure, by any means, Crappie George carried himself in a somewhat elegant manner. Resplendent in a dingy, well-worn three-piece dark blue business suit, topped with a bowler-type, turn-of-the-century hat, he somehow portrayed a man of bearing with a distant past dignity. Carrying fishing pole, wicker fish basket and a back-pack, his mission was to fish the back waters of our immediate island area for crappies. When his basket was full, he would reappear to take the next boat back to Portland where he would sell his catch to the Chinese community.

The mystery of Crappie George was that, upon arrival, with sparse salutations or other remarks, he would disappear into the lowlands irrespective of inclement weather, reappearing the second morning thereafter, with brimming basket to board the Steamer America on her Portland-bound stop about 9:00 a.m. As a boy of eight, I was always present

> *for his arrivals and departures, desperately wishing he*
> *would tell me something of his exploits. However, his*
> *closely guarded conversations were not forthcoming to a*
> *back country farm boy.*

The spring of 1930 came, warm and exciting, as events unfolded in my senior year. Historic family changes had taken place during the previous 12 months. Grandmother Sarah Elizabeth died and, 6 months later, Grandfather Bill passed on at age 84. Sarah was always a sweet and kindly lady to me. Bill passed us grandchildren by in his self-contained way never giving me much time or notice. On brief relaxed occasions, he would relate his duck, goose and swan shooting exploits as a young man. At those times he would also touch on his Chinook Indian linguistic capabilities interspersed with narrations of his Alaskan adventure during the gold rush of 1898.

As the end of the school year approached, great excitement prevailed as we decorated Florence Hall for the Senior Prom. I couldn't dance. Graduation day, May 28th, was also held at Florence Hall. There were 16 in my class of 1930. The ceremony opened with glowing remarks by Superintendent Stephen Smith, certain of which must have been made with tongue-in-cheek, because some of us boys made parts of the year less than comfortable for him. After passing out the diplomas, with selected diction he warmly introduced the principal speaker, Dr. Arnold Bennett Hall, University of Oregon's president, who presented a stirring address to the pitifully small assembly. Mother was terribly impressed, avowing afterwards that it just had to be the finest speech she had ever heard. She was proud too. Her only offspring was growing up following a sheltered, mostly rural adolescence.

A high school friend's father, Mr. Bill Gilkerson, oper-

Scappoose High School Shop Class

ated a small logging operation in the hills south of Scappoose. After graduation, he hired me, a totally un-qualified 17-year-old. My beginning job was unhooking the "choker" from the logs as they were pulled into the "cold-deck" (log pile), at the spar tree by the steam-don-key "yarder." The job paid $5.00 per day. Mother would have strongly objected to such employment had she had any knowledge of the hazards of the job.

My next job was sawing, with a Wade drag saw, and splitting 24-inch lengths of firewood for the firebox's enor-mous appetite of the yarder's steam boiler. As needed, Mr. Gilkerson would select a clear-grained fir log as a wood log making my job somewhat more bearable. Little did I know that in less than nine years, the drag saw's manu-facturer, R. M. Wade & Co. would be my employer for the next many years. That logging camp job, which I obtained entirely on my own initiative was my first job away from home. Lessons like "watch your step" and " use your head" were learned as I worked around heavy, dangerous tools and machinery.

By mid-summer 1930, with the grandparents gone, Dad by then had given up occupancy of the old Morgan's Landing Farm. The Morgan estate was divided amongst the heirs. The daughters, Aunt Elmina, Aunt Nettie, Aunt Daisey, Aunt Nell and Aunt Laura, becoming the heiresses to the home place consisting of about 540 acres, representing most of the original land grant square mile.

Dad's inherited share was approximately 210 acres just south of the main ranch. Uncle Alba's share was the most southerly 250 acres of the original 1000 acres. By 1948, 91 acres of Uncle Alba's portion would become Lucy Ann's and mine. Aunt Louella, at age 25, married Winfred Scott Copeland, age 29, January 1, 1907 in a dual ceremony when Aunt Laura, age 23, married Omar Corwin Spencer, age 26. After having operated Morgan's Landing Farm from about 1911, Aunt Lou and Uncle Win chose to take Aunt Lou's inheritance early in 1919 in the form of 120 acres half a mile north of the main ranch which Grandfather Bill had owned.

Following the family changes of 1930, Uncle Omar C. Spencer, a successful Portland attorney, began at once to arrange purchase of the Morgan daughters' shares, thereby holding the 540 acres and all buildings of the Morgan's Landing Farm intact.

With a complete renovation in 1935, the year electric power and telephones came, the great green-shuttered white house sparkled as it had when it was built in 1883. A sad final note occurred on a fall day in 1953 when the white house of so many memories was completely destroyed by fire, ending a part of the long history of the Morgan clan.

Now, as the last decade of the 20th century unfolds, all traces of Morgan land ownership on Sauvie Island are gone. Also, the Columbia has changed. The steamboats are only history and the Great River of The West, now subdued by myriad hydroelectric dams, has lost some of its elegant vitality.

Our 1918 Model E Buick 7-passenger touring car

My restoration of Dad Newton's last car, a 1949 6-cylinder Hudson 5-passenger coupe

PART TWO

A LARGER WORLD

After high school graduation in 1930, the prospects for a meaningful way of earning money with which to go to college were frighteningly elusive as the great U. S. depression worsened. Family ties, assets we all should value, made possible the opening of an important door for me.

A few years earlier, my cousin Helen Spencer had married Thomas Mahoney, Jr. Tom's father, the senior Mahoney, was a substantial businessman. Among other ventures, he held a mail hauling contract with the U. S. Postal service in Portland, Oregon. The contract involved moving all daily mail to and from trains, the airport, street car terminals, bus stations and Montgomery Ward & Co., the nation's premiere mail order house. In 1930 the main U. S. Post office building was located on west Broadway between west Glisan and Hoyt streets.

Cousin Tom Jr., knowing my desire to go to college, somehow prevailed upon his father to put me to work as a mail truck driver. At age seventeen my driving experience in city traffic was non-existent. My job was driving a one-ton hard-tired screened Moreland van, well identified in Post Office drab paint with gold lettering, in the downtown area from 2:00 p.m. to 11:30 p.m., five days a week, for $90.00 a month.

The Mahoneys having hired me was not well accepted by the other, older, experienced mail truck drivers. I felt they disapproved of a 17-year-old taking a job in those depression times when many family men were desperately looking for work. After a few months, when we all got acquainted, they finally recognized me as one of them. The U. S. mail job was my chance to save some money each month in preparation for starting at Oregon State College at Corvallis in September 1932. O.S.C. later became Oregon State University.

Friends to some of the Morgans, but barely known to Mother and Dad, the John Diefels, had a son, John Jr., who had just graduated from O. S. C. John, a polished graduate of muscular build and affable personality, took an interest the summer of '32 in apprizing me of the different world awaiting me as an O. S. C. freshman.

John Diefel Jr. sent my name to the inter-fraternity council and several fraternities mailed me invitations to visit them registration-rushing week. All fraternities were scratching to attract any potential pledge in those lean times, otherwise they never would have looked a second time at a 19-year-old country boy with little money, no attractive credentials and only a diploma from Scappoose High School, so remote it was barely identifiable in advanced-learning circles.

Having made good use of my fine model A Ford as I prepared for college, before going to Corvallis I left the car in the reliable hands of my good friend Frank L. Collins. Frank was a true friend, somewhat older, who upon graduation from high school chose the non-higher-education route. He went to work for the Pacific Telephone company at age 17. He worked up through the ranks never having had another employer. He and his beloved wife Isis were dedicated mates, always good citizens, who saw some lean times, raised a family and retired in comfort only to die comparatively young of natural causes.

It became obvious in 1933 that I could not afford to own the model A any longer. Frank wanted the car but could not obligate himself to buy it. Other newly married friends, Art and Bea Clifford, also wanting their first car, bought the little model A for $100.00 cash. Within one week after paying me, Art had an accident. Although he was unhurt, the fine little car that had meant so much to me was totally demolished.

As enrollment for my freshman year at O.S.C. approached, Dad and Mother drove me and my meager belongings to Corvallis on a fine September Sunday, dropping me off at the Alpha Tau Omega fraternity house where I had been invited to visit as a possible pledge. Dad handed me a $20.00 bill, wishing me all of the best, Mother shed a tear and I embarked on my quest for an education.

That was the only money Dad ever provided for me, as times were difficult for him since he had no regular job. I had saved $250.00 Post Office job dollars that got me started. Ever generous Great Aunt Nora Laue gave me $200.00 during that freshman year as I learned how to exist in a thinly drawn, competitive college environment.

After pledge-week invitations, meetings and dinners from the ATOs, Phi Delts, Betas and Phi Gs, I finally chose

Alpha Tau Omega fraternity house, Alpha Sigma Chapter,
Oregon State College, 1936

Alpha Sigma chapter of ATO and became what must have been their greenest pledge amongst some fourteen other freshmen.

Room and board was $35.00 per month. By some inscrutable means, I endured the first college year, didn't make the grade list for fraternity initiation, left in June for the summer, penniless and with no prospects for a job to earn money for the sophomore year. One of my ATO pledge brothers, Gordon Morris, blessed with great, financially stable parents, provided me with rides to and from school.

By 1933 Dad had used most of the proceeds from the sale to Uncle Omar Spencer, the previous year, of his inherited farm share. Dad had invested his limited cash reserves in a Southern Oregon quicksilver mining venture in consort with Uncle Win Copeland. The investment did not materialize profitably.

Dad and Mother were living very frugally in a modest rented house on Sauvie island in 1933, the absolute bottom point of the depression. I had no place to go but to live with them, finding only the most menial, occasional jobs. After a few unfruitful weeks that dismal summer, I located some ash tree stumpage and started sawing by hand and splitting ash cordwood. A cord in eight hours of hard labor was the best I could cut. I had a friend, Earnie Lonkie, who had a one and a half ton flatbed truck on which he could haul two cords per load into the Holman Fuel Company yard in Portland.

Earnie charged $3.00 per cord, hauling two cords per load to Holman Fuel Company in Portland. They paid me $7.00 per cord from which I had to pay Earnie's hauling charge. It was not a profitable summer and I went to Corvallis in the fall with little cash.

Once again good friendship paid dividends. One of my ATO sophomore classmates, Dick Larson, had obtained a job tending the college greenhouse boiler, 24 hours a day. The boiler room included a flat on the second floor large enough for two beds and an electric plate and sink. Dick asked me to join him in keeping the greenhouse at proper temperature. Just like that, I had a place to stay at no cost. We heated some food, occasionally, took some meals at the ATO house, and I waited tables elsewhere. The 1933-34 school year could not be described as anything but downright thin. My grades got better, however, and I was initiated early in the spring of 1934 as a full ATO member.

The summer of 1934 was another tough money period. Fall and my Junior year came with some much needed improvement at O.S.C. I was elected house manager. That meant room and board at the ATO house at no cost to me. I had developed some sorority contacts and soon got some table waiting assignments for special occasions. I completed the required basic military schooling and became eligible for the Reserve Officers Training Corps and enrolled as a second lieutenant. For a guy coming from next to nowhere, that officers uniform and high polished boots took me several steps forward in self-esteem.

The officers training also paid $15.00 per month. Being a farm boy, I knew how to ride horses. I thought I looked pretty sharp, in full uniform, astride an army horse on dress parade. We also did some fancy 4-horse team parade exercises, pulling a caisson and French 75 cannon on wheels.

One exercise, involving the entire field artillery unit included setting up a field command post on top of a small hill. I was in charge of installing some gun positions in the valley below. At one point in the exercise, the commanding officer at the post ordered me to bring gun emplacement detail on the double. My duty included a fast white army saddle horse. Per instructions, I took off from the valley at a fast gallop, arriving at the hilltop post pronto. I dismounted without concealing my white horse in natural cover, leaving it in view for miles in all directions. I got chewed-out, reprimanded and laughed at for such shortsightedness in full view of the make-believe enemy. My lack of procedural discipline became a mark against my internal grading. I never advanced above 2nd lieutenant.

RESERVE OFFICERS TRAINING EXERCISE

Upon enrolling at Oregon Agricultural College in 1932 as perhaps one of the greenest entrants of the year, I found that all Freshmen were required to sign up for ROTC, either in infantry or artillery. I chose the latter. Following the first year as a returning Sophomore, I could elect for training as a Second Lieutenant. It was easy to turn in the drab woolen "Private's" gear at the beginning of the second year in exchange for an "Officers" issue, trim jodh-

purs, riding boots and form fitting green jacket and jaunty visor cap.

The field artillery makeup of 1932 was not motorized. Officers rode horses. The caissons and French 75 cannons were four-horse drawn, too. For whatever else I lacked as a country boy, I did know horses and soon commanded a complete mobile caisson/French 75 four-horse drawn unit for all special field exercises. Elsewhere herein I have described my unfortunate exercise that contributed to keeping me from becoming a lst Lieutenant.

A driver of the team-pulled equipment rode the left lead horse. For exhibition, we did close-order drills at full gallop which, for me as a driver regaled in full officer's uniform, was exciting and challenging. My officer's allowance was $15.00 per month which, in those lean years, was most welcome.

The close-order gallop drills with caissons and field cannons were done in a pattern that formed an "X" in the center of the drilling field. Four drivers and teams with equipment running at full-gallop timed to meet and cross at the "X," requiring precise judgment of the oncoming-opposing team's speed as each converged at a 45-degree angle. The driver on the left lead horse arrived at the crossing point just a split second after the opposing French 75 gun had passed. The entire exercise was exciting to participate in and was also of great interest to spectators.

The ROTC program was one of the highlights for me in my over-all O.S.C. experience.

In the spring of my Junior year, I had become an advertising salesman for the Oregon State *Barometer* newspaper.

As my senior year started, after a dismal summer with little earnings, chemistry professor William Caldwell, a compassionate benefactor and ATO alum, loaned me $400.00.

That summer of 1935 prior to my senior term, my hopes had dashed so far as earning money was concerned. The quicksilver mine Dad had invested in had been obliged to cut back on full paid miners, but did have some openings for college boys at scaled-down pay. My cousin Jim Copeland and I took jobs there and spent the summer working at the mine as it convulsed in its financial death throes. We went there in June and worked through August on the promise of $5.00 per day and room and board, which was fine as long as the food lasted. Although we produced several 75 pound flasks of marketable mercury, we endured the last month with little food and no pay.

In spite of a busted summer, getting back to Corvallis for my senior year promised fair times and a certain element of excitement. With the loan from Professor Caldwell, I could plan payment for tuition and books. Again, being ATO house manager provided room and board. I started that fall as advertising manager of the Barometer which paid some. Certain perks went with the position. By some persuasion, I made arrangements for a city bus pass. The Memorial Union barbershop gave me free haircuts for turning business their way. Continuing officer's rank in the R.O.T.C. had its advantages too.

1936 came in with a slightly improved national economy and a host of promises for me although I concluded my senior year short on credits to graduate.

Just as things seemed to be closing out on the upturn, I got word from Dad and Mother, then living in Grants Pass, Oregon, that Mother was not doing well physically.

Although Mother looked frail, I just didn't realize that I would see her only once or twice more before she died on June 15th that year, at the incomprehensible early age of 48.

Shortly after returning to school from that weekend with my folks, I again was shocked to receive a phone call from Portland advising that my cousin Jack Spencer was missing and presumed drowned in the Columbia River. His empty motor launch had been sighted, drifting untended.

Again I took a bus, this time to Portland, and went directly to Morgan's Landing Farm, then owned and operated by my Uncle Omar and Aunt Laura Spencer. Upon my arrival, I found them frantically managing a civilian search for their son Jack. I spent the weekend with them before returning to Corvallis. Jack's body was found three days later, four miles downstream from the ranch.

The tragedy of Jack's untimely death at age 26 had completely overcome Uncle Omar. He had built the farm up to a beautiful state primarily in an attempt to make something attractively permanent for Jack, who had done little with his prior life. Deluged by his loss, my Uncle pleaded with me to come to the farm as soon as school was over to be with him until he could somehow sort out his feelings about the future of the lovely farm property that meant so much to him, to me and the entire family.

At school's end I immediately went to the farm. Within two weeks, Mother passed away while in the care of Aunt Mary Laue.

Circumstances not seeming to coincide with my original desire, which was to leave O.S.C. with a degree, I settled on going to the ranch. As a hard worker, earning $50.00 a month, having fine living conditions and the good, down-home cooking of Mrs. Lillie Oatman, the housekeeper of Spencer's Farm, I felt good about the immediate future.

Some of the hurts caused by cousin Jack's death began to heal, and Uncle Omar made every attempt to turn over operation of the farm to me. He had another hired man, Reynolds Baumgartner. With me taking the lead on all jobs, we got a lot done. Making 500 tons of meadow grass hay which had to be stored in the two barns took about 6 weeks of that first summer. Extra farmhands were hired then too.

The fall of 1936, Uncle Omar was so pleased with the

fine hay we had put up, he decided to buy 300 head of bred Hereford beef cows from Montana. Twenty-five percent of the herd had horns and all had to be branded. Reynolds was no hand with horses, which left the wrangling and such bloody work as de-horning those cows to me. The beef cow project went well and we settled into the winter of '36-'37 feeding 300 head of cattle twice a day, and cleaning the barns of all that manure once a month.

Uncle Omar bought a new 1938 Ford pick-up for the farm and I had the privilege of using it some in the off hours. In the winter, when daytime work was light, I would drive into Portland every other Wednesday afternoon, pick up a load of farm supplies and feed for the work horses, dairy-cows and the large flock of laying hens that Mrs. Oatman tended. I would stay in town for dinner with friends and get back to the ranch before the Burlington Ferry stopped service at 1:00 a.m. The Spencers always came to the farm over a long weekend. After work on Saturdays, I could often use their always late-model Buick for a night on the town.

By early spring of 1937 Uncle Omar and I were spending a lot of time together, mostly making substantial farm plans. I had learned enough about irrigation at the Oregon State College farms, and was anxious to try irrigation on some of the ranch sandy soils. Uncle Omar was so anxious to see farm progress, he was agreeable to most of my suggestions, with little concern for the costs.

By April of 1937, he gave me permission to build and install a trial irrigation system on about 5 acres of heavy sandy soil. The project involved designing and building a permanent pumping station out into the Columbia River. That structure necessitated doing a design plan and getting approval for the construction from the U. S. Corps of Engineers to build a pump installation 60 feet out from the shore of that navigable stream.

I did the design, obtained the permit, engaged a pile-driver contractor to drive four pairs of fir piling at 20-foot intervals and install 12-inch by 12-inch by 14-foot timber caps on each piling pair and secure each cap with drift-bolts. Once that foundation work was done, I then prepared to lay 6-inch by 10-inch by 22-foot fir stringers in place, crossways of the caps.

Thus was the pump dock frame extended out from the river shore about 60 feet. I next placed decking of 2-inch by 12-inch by 8-foot planking crossways of the stringers to complete a very stable dock walkway and base for a turbine pump placement. We then had installed a 7 and a half horsepower electric line-shaft turbine pump with 30 feet of column and shaft, submerging the bowl assembly in several feet of water. I plumbed in a 4-inch discharge pipeline from the pump to shore along the edge of the dock decking, connecting it with the newly set up overhead sprinkler irrigation system.

That project involved a type of engineering design and construction I felt competent to accomplish mostly as a result of my college formal and practical education. The revelation of irrigation water being applied to parched soil, with resultant seed germination and related plant growth, new to me, would in two short years become the cornerstone for my 50-year life's work in the irrigation industry.

The vigor of youth generates the impetus to tackle most any kind of project. The oldest large cattle barn on the ranch, known as #1, was 120 feet long and 70 feet wide. Its foundation framework was imbedded in newly pumped-in sand from dredging operations to clean the Columbia River channel. Only the barn's foundation beams were left exposed. The entire structure needed to be raised a few inches to preserve its foundation framework.

Uncle Omar and I discussed the magnitude of raising a structure of such proportions. I concluded that we could elevate the barn ourselves, even though I had no previous experience of raising anything larger or more complex than an umbrella. Uncle Omar said, "Let's do it."

Prior to that time I had never even seen a building jack. I talked with two building movers and learned from the discussions how to proceed with the barn raising project. I calculated the number of jacks needed and proceeded to rent 72 of them for a month. Each jack weighed about 50 pounds. I had to make two pick-up loads to get them all on site.

Much digging ensued as Reynolds and I exposed each beam underside and placed all 72 jacks. We then hand-screwed each jack, slowly elevating the entire barn 16 inches. After placing new concrete footings and posts at 10-foot intervals, we backed off each jack until the full weight of the barn rested on the new footings, placing its underside well above the sand.

Building the irrigation pump dock out into the river and raising barn #1 were two big projects that each turned out well. After having been on the ranch almost a year, Uncle Omar raised my pay to $75.00 per month. Within that period, I had paid back the $400 that Professor Caldwell had loaned me while in school.

THE GRANGE

The Patrons of Husbandry, as the Grange was known, was an association of farmers, organized in the United States in 1867 for mutual welfare and advancement of human understanding.

Oliver H. Kelley, a New Englander, had settled on a farm near Itasca, Minnesota. Later, moving to Washing-

ton D.C., he became employed as a clerk in the Department of Agriculture, being sent through the Southern states to survey agricultural conditions. He was stricken by what he called "a lack of progressive spirit" among the agricultural classes. The idea came to him of organizing farmers into a fraternal association. In 1867, with six other men, he formed the Patrons Of Husbandry, later to become known as the National Grange. He continued the organizational work, emphasizing the "social, intellectual and fraternal" benefits of the order. Others saw the Grange as a way to attack the burgeoning "Co-operative" monopolies that were thought to be oppressing farmers. The organization flourished, a landmark in cooperative effort, an example of the power of united public endeavors.

By 1912 cooperative farmers organizations impelled the Grange into the Co-operative marketing business, its half million members united in a political and economic program that startled the nation.

The Grange was first active on my native Sauvie Island only briefly in the late 1800s, as a community fraternal group, mostly because of the lack of communication in the days before passable roads and telephones. A determined group of principled Sauvie Islanders, seeking the benefits and social aspects of the Grange, re-organized an Island Chapter of Patrons Of Husbandry in the early 1930s.

In 1936, I went to live and work on Morgan's Landing Farm for Uncle Omar C. Spencer, who was always an enthusiastic Granger. He soon prevailed on me to join the Sauvie Island Grange and participate in the new community spirit resulting therefrom.

My Oregon State College training, rural boyhood and the then current desire to explore and demonstrate the latest agricultural advancements, including sprinkler irrigation, made me a qualified and enthusiastic potential Grange member, and I joined. Within a year, having gone through the "chairs" of the secret Grange organization, I became the Island Chapter Worthy Master. Following my term, I was awarded the "Past Masters" emblematic badge in the winter of 1937. With overflowing pride, prior to our en-

gagement announcement, I pinned the coveted emblem of the Grange on my future mate for all of the years to come, dearest Lucy Ann Wendell, to wear until we could choose her selected engagement ring.

As Lucy Ann and I planned our marriage, Uncle Omar's imagination and effervescent sense of humor generated a Grange highlight of unique proportions for us. With great pre-planning, the Grange chapter produced a Mock Wedding in our honor, capped with the presentation to us of a beautiful silver serving tray with a lovely inscription of Grangers' well-wishes. The night of the Mock Wedding was bundled fun and much laughter as Uncle Omar's script was portrayed by certain members. The "Bride" (Ima Whale) played by corpulent old friend Walter Graf was the center of much mirth. The "Groom" (Ivan Awful-Itch) was done by Gene Snyder, who worked for Uncle Omar. Uncle played the part of the ceremonial Jewish Rabbi to perfection. He reveled in the evening's pointed fun.

Thus my Grange experience is worthy of many memories including the love shown by my Patrons Of Husbandry peers. It was yet another hallmark phase in my early life.

As the fall of 1937 approached, unforseen romantic changes in my life were destined to occur. One day my good friends Frank and Isis Collins suggested I come in to town for a movie and a blind-date with a girl Isis said I just must meet. After all, I was then 24 and floating.

The date was Lucy Ann Wendell, a girl who worked with Isis at Lipman Wolfe & Co. department store on Fifth and Alder Streets. Lucy Ann was fun and easy to talk with. The first date led to another. On our the third date, as we sat in the pick-up at the entrance to the King Albert Apartments where she lived, I mustered enough nerve for the first kiss.

Lucy Ann and I continued to have dates. Getting better acquainted, I learned of the disruptive years she expe-

Lucy Ann Wendell Morgan

rienced when both her parents died within a couple of years, leaving her at age 14 to live with Aunt Estella, a wonderful woman who also had experienced many rough spots in her life.

"Wendy," as Lucy Ann has often been called, and I had more and more dates and fun with our mutual friends the Collins, the brothers Sloan and their wives, the Smiths and Blackstones. Trips to the mountains and rather customary Saturday night gatherings for bridge and such, nicely filled our time.

The winter of 1937-38 again was one of the coldest. The Columbia River was choked with floating ice. A big snow storm started on Sunday afternoon, February lst. By 8:00 a.m. February 2nd, Portland was blanketed with 14 inches, the latest heavy snowfall of record. By the spring of 1938, Wendy and I had gotten closer to serious talks of what life for us would be if we married.

In August of 1938, we visited Heitkemper's Jewelers in Portland where Wendy selected her engagement ring. Aunt Dorothy Johnson held a lovely engagement party for Wendy at the pretty Johnson home on Floral Avenue in Laurelhurst. Aunt Dorothy's home would be the center of much activity in the coming months as the wedding date of December 10th grew nearer.

Prior to the wedding that year, in the late summer of 1938 as marital plans were taking precedence over most everything else, I was still working at the ranch. I felt I needed to come to some conclusions with Uncle Omar about my continued participation in the operation of Morgan's Landing Farm. It was a typical Sunday morning walk around the ranch, an event that Uncle Omar thoroughly enjoyed. The past two years had seen a close uncle-nephew bond having developed between us.

I can recall almost the exact spot where we were walking. I had given a lot of thought as to just how to approach Uncle Omar on the vital matter of my continuing work association with him. At that long-ago moment I said, "Uncled Omar, we have done a lot of constructive things here on the ranch these past two years. What can I look forward to if I stay on with you?" He quickly replied, "Bob, our farm relationship has been fine, but frankly I have no plans for you in the foreseeable future because I am still trying to determine the destiny of the ranch."

Since this sincere revelation came as I was considering marriage, I reckoned it was, to some extent, a good omen. It seemed that now I must earnestly seek some sort of trade employment. Wendy was a city girl and for her early married life, being thrust into a farm life environment may have been difficult for her. I felt it was time for me to meet the challenges of the business world. Shortly after my serious talk with Uncle Omar, I told him I was preparing to look for a city job.

That summer, I had purchased a fine used 1936 Chevy coupe from Warren Braley of Braley-Graham Buick in Portland. Warren was going with Wendy's good friend

Dodo Wolfe, soon to become Warren's wife.

The Chevy was a good stable vehicle having been driven but 18,000 miles. It gave me a feeling of stability, even though I only squeezed by on meager and somewhat insecure pay-scheduling at Pacific Co-op, my first city employer.

With contacts having been made, I soon found an opportunity to work in the warehouse of Pacific Supply Cooperative at 16th and West Hoyt Streets in Portland. It was not much of a job, but it challenged my thoughts on matters of earning a living.

Marriage plans came on fast in the fall as we approached the pre-set date of December 10th. Wendy had enough money to plan and put on the kind of wedding she had always hoped for. Aunt Dorothy's full support and enthusiastic cooperation made all the preparations a joy for Wendy.

Marriage to the grandest girl of all occurred amidst all of the fanfare, glitter, best wishes and gifts anyone could dream

My bride, Lucy Ann (Wendy)

of. The wedding ceremony was celebrated at Grace Memorial Episcopal Church followed by a great reception, again at Aunt Dorothy's. It was one of those typically foggy late fall Portland nights. It was so foggy, in fact, that we spent our first married night a short drive away in Vancouver, Washington. On Sunday, we continued as we had planned to Seaside, Oregon.

The year of our marriage was economically bland. I knew very little about doing business. By some means, however, I did arrange to take possession of an apartment on 20th and West Overton one week prior to our December 10th wedding. It was meager under any circumstances. The front door opened into a mini-parlor, about 10 feet by 10 feet. The small kitchen was through an opening to the right. From the front door across the living room was a miniature bedroom beyond which was an equally unimpressive bathroom. The 355-square-foot apartment rented for $25.00 a month. After existing there for about four months, we moved west two blocks to a slightly larger apartment, up one flight of stairs where Lucy, now pregnant, found such stairs a challenge.

Fortunately, among the many lovely wedding gifts was a check for $25.00 from dear Great Aunt Nora Laue. It represented the greatest portion of our first month's reserve. Wendy was earning $75.00 per month at Lipman-Wolfe and I was being spasmodically paid something less at the Co-op.

In the spring of the year before, in 1937, when I was looking at pump and irrigation suppliers, I had talked seriously with the pump department manager, Crawford Reid, about buying from R. M. Wade & Company. However, we eventually chose to buy from California Culvert Company, one of Uncle Omar's law clients. Even so, Crawford and I maintained contact.

About one week after the wedding, I was surprised to receive a call from Crawford Reid suggesting that if I were interested, R. M. Wade & Co. was considering hiring an irrigation equipment salesman to sell their newly established system known as Wade Rain. I jumped at the opportunity to discuss the job with Crawford. Our meeting was a good one and Crawford set up a final meeting with Wade Newbegin, president of R. M. Wade & Co., for, as I recall, December 18, 1938. All details of the job were discussed and we agreed that I would start my new career December 26th. I would work on a straight commission contract, drawing $125.00 per month against earned commissions. I would pay all of my own business expenses, furnishing my own car as well.

Looking back, it was not much, but times would get even more lean. By January, Wendy found she was pregnant and was obliged to leave her job at Lipmans the end of February 1939 as we looked forward with excitement to our first baby in September.

On a Saturday night, some two weeks before Daniel's arrival, our good friends, the brothers Al and Brud Sloan and wives, Frank and Isis Collins and the Glenn Blackstones had a party, celebrating the impending birth date.

With good fun and jokes, we had great times. Employed as I was at R. M. Wade & Co., which sold many types of home water pumps, I had found, in rummaging around amongst some out-dated basement inventory, a strange looking, unused hand pump fashioned to pump liquids from a fifty gallon barrel. As a joke, I had put the pump in the trunk of my car and the night of the party, amongst all of the camaraderie, I excused myself, went out to the car, got the pump, and walked into the house carrying the odd looking contraption. Immediately I was barraged with questions. Following the fusillade of queries, I quickly explained that though I knew little about events leading up to our first birth, I was just trying to be prepared for impending realities. What I had was my version of a "Ready Beddy Pump." The laughing and clamor fixed the entire group into an ever more jovial mood for the rest of that memorable evening.

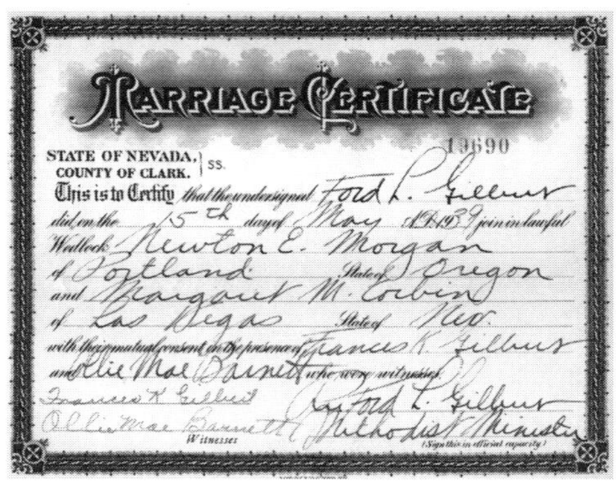

Marriage Certificate, Newton E. Morgan and Margaret M. Corbin

More important changes formed on the family horizon the spring of 1939. Dad, who had grieved over Mother's death in 1936, had returned to Salinas, California. Later he had spent quite a lot of time with his sister, Aunt Nettie at her home in Monrovia, California, into 1938. He had made a special trip to Portland when Lucy and I were married, and then returned to California. Following his return to Aunt Nettie's, Dad was feeling more lonely and was anxious for companionship. Providence was at work. Immediately across the street from Aunt Nettie's, a neighbor's divorced sister was visiting. By whatever circumstances, the neighbor's sister, Margaret Matilda Schuler, and Dad became acquainted. They saw a lot of each other the spring of 1939, and were soon married.

Demure, fastidious Stepmother Margaret was a jewel and immediately became the perfect mate for Dad, fitting into the Morgan family with a perfection of her own styling.

One hundred and twenty-five dollars a month went a long way In 1939. Besides supporting all our living costs, our nice Chevy had to carry me at least 500 miles each week as I travelled from Vancouver, Washington to the Canadian border in western Washington and back, developing sales of Wade Rain sprinkler irrigation systems which included pulling the demonstration Wade Rain trailer at least 50 percent of the time.

Seeking out farmers interested in irrigation, setting up the demonstration system, powered by a 9-horsepower air-cooled engine that propelled a 1.5-inch discharge centrifugal pump, in the snow or rain, on a western Washington March day, presented some sales challenges that Dale Carnegie never encountered.

There was a farmers co-operative in Vancouver that I found I could join for $5.00, which included one share of stock. Members were privileged to buy supplies, including petroleum products at a substantial discount. My cost on gasoline was 11 cents per gallon. Each Monday morning, as I headed north through Vancouver, I would stop by the Co-op and take on 35 gallons of gasoline, which would last most of the week. Case lots of canned goods were also a bargain at the Co-op. Canned cherries and peaches became a substantial part of our diet.

By the late summer of 1939, as we anticipated our first born's arrival, some very nice things came our way. About the first of September, in accordance with my Wade contract, commissions were paid for my first season's work. I had earned over $900.00 above my monthly drawing account. By then, we had left the Bungalow Court Apartments and a second interim apartment, and were prepared to move into a nice five-room bungalow with full basement. It was owned by Adelaide and Mike Frye, close friends of Aunt Dorothy and Uncle Mel.

The rent was $35.00 a month. Ad Frye ranks among the neat ladies in our lives, having done many nice things for us as we set up serious housekeeping for the first time. In our second married year, with a bank account exceeding anything we might have imagined, we prepared to buy basic furniture for our dandy rented house.

Commercial and Home Furnishers, a broker Wendy learned of through a friend, provided us, for a price, foundation furnishings including a Duncan-Fife dining room table and four chairs, sofa and ottoman, coffee, drum-top and swing top occasional tables. All of this, except for the coffee table, after over 55 years, is still part of our everyday furniture. A double bed was included; however, it and a beautiful new Coldspot refrigerator have long since been replaced.

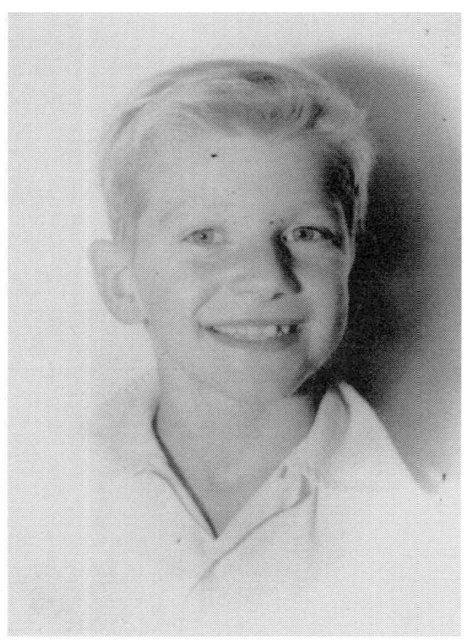

Daniel Munro Morgan

On September 14th, a hot autumn day, Wendy delivered Daniel Munro Morgan, our first-born, at St. Vincent's Hospital. There was no air-conditioning then, but the new young mothers, all part of the six-bed maternity ward, didn't seem to notice the heat in the euphoria of becoming moms.

Danny was a charmer and he and his ecstatic parents settled into our rather well appointed home, with a completely supplied nursery provided from the many "showers" held for Wendy.

The next years flew by for our little family. Dad and Margaret built a cute new house in Sunnyside, Oregon, adjacent to the old David Hunter family farm which held some of my most cherished childhood memories. By then, my trusted Chevy had accumulated many miles. We bought our first new car, a Ford V8 deluxe four-door sedan. A big step up for us.

The winter of 1940-41 resounded with disturbing rumblings in Western Europe as German dictator Adolph Hitler opened conquests with his ruthless, sabered minions.

Domestically, things for Wendy, Daniel and me were going just wonderfully, even though Danny was bothered with a tenacious skin problem far too long.

In 1941, on a mid-summer morning, following another successful irrigation-selling season, as I returned to our 21st street home in Westmoreland from playing golf, I swung through beautifully landscaped Eastmoreland. On Crystal Springs Boulevard, I turned north onto 32nd Avenue and set off a series of events leading to another step forward in our lives. As I drove slowly down the street, I observed a "for sale" sign in the yard of a brand new red brick house that surely looked good from the street.

When I got home, I described the house on 32nd to Wendy, suggesting that we go look at it. The builder showed us the overwhelmingly attractive interior and Wendy and I began trying to figure how we could possibly acquire such a lovely home. We were inspired, but then looked at other houses in the same area, always coming back to the 32nd Avenue red brick jewel.

The sale price was $6,600.00. We prepared to finance and buy the house. In early September, we moved in. Once settled in our fine new home on 32nd Avenue in Eastmoreland, we kept very busy as we awaited our second born, son John Wesley Morgan, who arrived at 11 p.m. on October 28, 1941, the evening of Portland's first "black-

Our first-owned house on Eastmoreland in Portland, Oregon

out" alert. It was also the night that I finished a five-week Dale Carnegie sales training course.

Being a 28-year-old father of two, employed by a war effort supplier, I was deferred from the military draft, relegated to civilian night patrol duty in sensitive areas. Irrigation system lay-out and design was classified as a war effort enterprise enhancing production of food and fiber.

Our third born, Mary Ann, arrived September 19th, 1944 in the dark days of World War II. However, the joys of a cute blonde daughter brightened our lives with exciting brilliance.

Cousins William and his wife Norma Morgan, living in Pendleton, Oregon, invited us one year to bring the family for a visit. By then, Mary Ann was blossoming, too. We would all go camping at Wallowa Lake in the vastness of Oregon's Wallowa Mountains, and then return back to their home for the opening of the famed Pendleton Happy Canyon and Round-Up, a Wild West Show. Bill and Norma's daughter Joyce and Mary Ann developed a "cousin bond" on that trip.

Late one summer, probably in 1946, on a Sunday, our family of now five was expecting the arrival of yet unnamed James. We had just returned from one of our many fun outings, and I was obliged to make one of our many emergency junkets to the hospital, this time with John. Somehow, so soon after World War II, when unessential goods were still hard to get, among my many factory connections, we were able to purchase a very nice, all aluminum tricycle for him. We no sooner had unpacked the car and entered our fine Eastmoreland home when John rolled his new tricycle out of the garage, zipped down the driveway at high speed, made a quick John-style right turn, and crashed onto the cement sidewalk. Up he came with a sizeable chin laceration, spewing blood all over. He and I spent the next two hours in Emergency as the staff administered a stitching job on him.

James Wendell was born to us on September 17th, 1947, a fine, always good and happy boy whose arrival rounded out our family of six. By then, two years had passed since the war and I was deeply involved in developing Wade Rain portable sprinkler irrigation business across the United States.

My aptitude for new challenges led me to think more and more about acquiring a farm, selling our Eastmoreland home and raising our family in rural surroundings. Just how "rural" my selection would turn out to be would soon cause me to wonder why I had chosen to subject Wendy to the rigors of a spartan farm life while she was married to a career traveler.

Uncle Alba Morgan, Dad's only brother, still retained 90.3 acres remaining from his Morgan's Landing Farm inheritance. It was bordered on the east by 1450 feet of Columbia River shoreline and an equal footage of the county road on the west. A simple five-room cabin with no

The Robert Morgan farm home, Sauvie Island, 1955 view

plumbing and a large unfinished nine-room salt-box-type frame house, only 60 percent completed, stood forlorn on a knoll, hurting from the ravages of fifteen harsh Western Oregon winters. Reached by a private dirt road a quarter-mile long, the land, about 50 percent cleared, had no electricity, domestic water or telephone service.

Although Wendy had no country experience, she raised no objections to acquiring such a property, and on April 15, 1948, we became the proud owners of the described land for $20,000.00.

We continued to live in Eastmoreland that beautiful Oregon spring, one of the nicest I could remember following a long, harsh winter in which the compacted snow levels in the vast Columbia and Snake River watersheds contained the highest water contents of record.

By early May of 1948, I had seeded about 30 acres to malting barley, my first crop on our very own land. A persistent northwestern United States warm weather pattern, starting in late April and increasing in intensity as the weeks went by, brought on the second highest flood conditions in the histories of the great river basins. By May 31st, the dike that protected the lowlands of most of Sauvie Island, including all the land of the original Morgan's Landing Farm, was strained to the most extreme limits. Standing at 31 feet above sea-level against the dike, which was designed to be 32 feet high but which had settled through the years as much as two feet, the ferocious Columbia tried both man and the land. Near our farm, the dike had settled and only expeditious placement of two tiers of sand-bags stood between us and disaster. Seepage behind the dike deluged most of our 90.3 acres and lingered six weeks after the river crested and receded, destroying most of my barley planting.

At the apex of the flood, with the lowlands swamped with seepage, all of the area farmers were forced to abandon their farms and move their livestock and belongings to high ground. Although I had grown up on the shore of the Columbia, our first year of land ownership taught me many things, including neighbor togetherness, lessons in other's heroism and individual concerns in times of stress. It was a time when we took stock of our beings and counted our blessings in the face of adversity.

THE SPRING OF 1948 COLUMBIA RIVER FRESHET
Some of Its Effects on Sauvie Island

Morgan's Landing Farm, owned by Omar Corwin Spencer, my uncle, was verdant and blossoming in late April of 1948. His fine high-production pure-bred Holstein dairy herd of some ninety cows, ably tended by Walter Graf, was producing at maximum as the spring meadow grasses grew thick and succulent.

That early spring in the vast Columbia River watershed which included the mighty Snake, together with the Okanogan and Yakima rivers, had been cold and backward with build-ups of record snow levels in the Western Rockies and Cascade Ranges. Official flood warnings had been posted daily as May arrived with a strong warming trend and intermittent heavy rains throughout the northwestern United States.

The Columbia River flood stage at Vancouver, Washington, of sixteen feet had been exceeded by May 12th. From that date, the river system had become ominous, rising another twelve feet by May 26th. The well-built dike surrounding approximately twelve thousand of the Island's southern-most acres, flanked by the Columbia and Willamette Rivers and the Multnomah Channel, was withstanding the freshet onslaught. Suddenly, evacuation of livestock, machinery and residents from low-lying areas immediately became urgent.

Uncle Omar and Walter Graf reacted quickly and prepared to move the valuable dairy herd and equipment to high ground, upstream near Troutdale, Oregon, just east of the Portland airport. Without hesitation, they engaged the services of Shaver Transportation Company's historic sternwheel steamboat, the <u>Henderson</u>, towing a huge empty Hog-Fuel barge of ample deck space to accommodate ninety cows.

This somewhat unusual flotilla, stemming the Columbia's swift currents, came ashore at a Morgan's Landing Farm beach site to take aboard the reluctant, nervous cows. Stocky Walter Graf, with lifetime herdsman's skills, selected a patient, quiet cow and persuaded her to climb a hastily constructed, steep gangway rising about twelve feet up to the barge deck. As Walter and the cow climbed the gangway, the rest of the herd timidly, yet obediently followed until all were loaded.

The entire procedure, taking place on a Saturday morning when the river level stood at 29 feet, was heavy with a seeming air of impending disaster. No one could know what lay ahead. To me, the efforts of Walter and his men comprised a noble feat worthy of strong praise under most try-

ing circumstances.

Memorial Day, 1948, was crystal clear and warm. At Morgan's Landing Farm, with all of the livestock and related dairy machinery gone, there was little to do as the river exceeded the 30-foot stage. So, we patrolled the dike and speculated when the river would crest. A handful of us, ever watching the water gauge, noted at 4:25 p.m. an unexplainable level drop of two and one-half inches. Without a radio or a telephone, we could not realize that the sudden drop resulted from a calamity of mammoth proportions.

At precisely 4:17 p.m., a dike surrounding several thousand acres across the Columbia River from Vancouver and adjacent to north Portland had broken, suddenly flooding the housing community of Vanport City. In a matter of less than an hour, the community of 9,943 buildings, housing 42,000 people, was deluged.

Henry J. Kaiser's gigantic construction enterprise had built Vanport City in less than a year, starting in 1942, at a cost of $26,000,000, to house many of his shipyard workers. They built four classes of wartime craft: Liberty ships, Victory ships, oil tankers and intermediate-sized aircraft carriers. The construction of these ships required the employment of over 75,000 workers. Kaiser's greatest effort was the "keel-to-launch" of the victory ship J. N. Teal in 14 working days.

The life of Vanport city for five and one-half years, and its violent death on May 30, 1948, portrayed a poignant chapter in the massive efforts to supply American support during World War II.

That unusual year, the Columbia crested above 31 feet, receding very little for another 30 days. Finally, Uncle's herd was brought back in early July. The freshet had brought unparalleled heartbreak and miseries to many good people.

My position at R. M. Wade & Co. kept me extremely busy. On days off, I energetically made plans for our new farm adventure. Mid-summer of 1949 found Wendy and me listing our fine Eastmoreland home for sale, an experience of six days duration. It sold for almost three times our original investment, causing us to move quicker than anticipated to temporary residence in a nice little bungalow on Uncle Omar's farm as re-construction progressed on the big house on our newly acquired farm.

We moved in November 12, a typically stormy Western Oregon day. Within two months, by January 5, 1950, the coldest weather ever recorded, minus 12 degrees on our back porch three successive mornings, plus 14 inches of snow, conditioned us in our new farm house. That weather, followed by a sleet storm that downed phone and power lines for two weeks, tested Wendy's and my collective ingenuities as we scurried to keep some semblance of warmth with the big house fireplace, central oil stove and kitchen trash burner. My time had been so completely consumed the previous fall, I had not stored a supply of firewood in a dry place and I was obliged to dig wood out of the snow and ice daily.

With all of the first two-year farm experiences behind us, meeting each new challenge, we henceforth enjoyed a comfortable, well equipped home, centered on an ever-increasingly profitable farm. We first stocked our 90.3 acres with sheep, for which Wendy characteristically developed an attachment. The boys exhibited lambs as 4-H entries at the Multnomah County Fair. We had purchased a registered Columbia ram that produced fine progeny. Mary Ann, in her traditional finery, was pictured on the front page of the morning *Oregonian* holding a newly born Hampshire-Columbia Cross lamb as she sat on a bale of straw.

Subsequently we developed a fine herd of Hereford short-horn beef cows to which we introduced "Junior," our double-registered polled Hereford bull that sired elegantly proportioned calves, worthy of the breed.

The children's enthusiastic involvement with the farm animals, the bucolic scenes of Hereford cows grazing on lush irrigated pastures, and our farm setting blending nicely with the beauty of the Columbia River environs, all contributed to the envisioned contentment I must have trusted would somehow become a reality when we initially chose that rural plan.

Mary Ann Morgan, age 7

The good times of our family-life, the winter evenings as we gathered around a roaring fireplace fire to enjoy crisp "Northern Spy" apples, the wholesome Saturday-morning French toast and country sausage breakfasts, community Grange gatherings and 4-H and "Future Farmers" activities, interspersed with ice-skating when the ponds froze over, all made for unforgettable formulative years for our growing family.

It must have been December, 1951, when, with all pre-arrangements having been made with Dad and Margaret, our family of six stuffed ourselves into the family Ford sedan and took off on a motoring trip to spend Christmas with the Grandparents at their home in Hemet, California, twelve hundred miles away.

Starting early the first morning following over-nighting

in Medford, Oregon, we crossed into California and soon were approaching beautiful Mt. Shasta. Rounding a promontory as we rolled along Interstate 5, we suddenly came upon a stunning view of the sunlit grandeur of majestic Mt. Shasta. Stopping at a strategic viewpoint, we all got out to drink in the magic of the mountain.

It was at that precise moment that James, then four years old, voiced his first soul-searching eloquence as he marveled at Mt. Shasta's beauty. He turned to his Mother and queried, "Mom, do I own myself?" The older boys, by then in their teens, simply cracked up, getting a great laugh from their young brother's innocent appraisal of presence before the magnitude of nature.

Margaret and Dad had everything planned, and they showed the family a great time. It must have been taxing for them, with our two teenagers, and so many appetites to satisfy. After Christmas and the goodbyes at Dad's and Margaret's, we spent a day and a night in Glendora with the LaFetras before wending our way north up Highway 101 for a night with George and Mary Ann Hattie in San Marino. Then we headed on

Dad and Margaret

back into Oregon and our farm home. It was a typically nice vacation trip during which the children saw so many new and interesting sights.

During the expanding years of the fifties, when extra business perks were commonplace in contrast with their near non-existence today, Wendy and I had some most enjoyable train trips with the same luxury features enjoyed by earlier generations during the Roaring Twenties. We particularly remember boarding the Great Northern's Chicago Limited in Portland, about 6:00 in the evening. Freshening up in a parlor suite before dinner at 7:30 p.m. in the sleek new dining car, replete with white linen tablecloths and the ever-in-place Portland rose in crystal vase, plus gleaming silver settings, was an awfully nice way for the country-boy and his beautiful blonde wife to relax after a busy day. A full day's travel and then another lovely dinner, as we sped east of Rapid City, North Dakota, then a second night in our freshly made-up bedroom was followed by our arrival in the Chicago outskirts. Our pullman would then soon arrive at the LaSalle station about 7:30 a.m. From there, we would re-embark for a destination, perhaps New York, Miami or New Orleans. Railroading has now lost its glamour, but for several years after 1950, we quite often had that never diminishing pleasure of a relaxed travel experience.

Family values take a priority stance in much of our present day society. Family participation commanded a front position as Daniel approached his senior high school year at Scappoose High. As the fall advanced to early winter, it became clear that Scappoose had a winning basketball team. Dan was the team manager. As the excitement mounted, we rarely missed a game. Wendy, in her usual gracious manner, invited the entire team and coaches to the farm for a grand Morgan festive dinner one weekend.

As the season progressed, Scappoose basketball fever mounted. The team surmounted all opponents through the play-offs and went to the Eugene finals, where they won the Oregon State Championship. Our family was completely involved in that winter of basketball supremacy. It was a great experience for Dan as one of the team. He, too, was awarded the coveted "Orange S."

The intricacies and demands of earning a living caused further stirring in my mind after having worked for R. M. Wade & Co. for eighteen years. In early 1957, I began planning a big change. My employer, a closely-held company, which meant no employee stock ownership and with no pension or retirement program, could only wish me well when I announced that I would seek other means of earning a living.

I had earlier negotiated and shortly agreed to buy a one-third interest in Cascade Tractor & Implement Co., a John Deere dealership in McMinnville, Oregon, courthouse seat of historic Yamhill County.

Having tendered my resignation with R. M. Wade & Co., we closed down the farm, offering it for sale. On June 15th, with reluctance and tears, particularly from James, the family bid the farm goodbye and moved with household possessions to a newly purchased home in McMinnville.

This new venture in business management was an energy-packed high point for me. After 18 years as an employee of R. M. Wade & Co., and the pace expected of a National Sales Manager, I was ready for a home-based, localized adventure at running a business where I was one of the owners.

Our farm home and acreage had not been sold. A medium-sized national recession had set in. Learning the vagaries of retailing to farmers, taking in used machinery trades without losing some of the minimal 23% gross John Deere margin of profit, all absorbed and tested me to the limit. The family had its share of good times while also being tested by teenage tribulations.

After we had moved to McMinnville and Dan had joined the U.S. Air Force, we took the rest of our brood to Seattle for the World's Fair. A lively time when, again, the young ones were introduced to some of the world's bright spots, so totally new to them.

Back in McMinnville, population 9,000 plus, we settled in to a small-town lifestyle that was new, but quickly assimilated in the children's thinking. John took to the bigger high school environment, including football and all of the associated events. Mary Ann fitted in, as would be expected, making many girlfriends, becoming part of Rainbow Girls, enjoying every minute. Jim, with his athletic tendencies, at age 10 became addicted to basketball, thanks to the backboard we installed on the garage-front at our home on Thompson Lane. Wendy tended the family and home and embarked on new involvements in her Christian Science Church activities.

Time went by ever more rapidly. A friend told me of the whereabouts, near Goldendale, Washington, 170 miles east of McMinnville, of a reasonably preserved 1917 model E6 Buick seven passenger touring car that could be had for $200.00. Intrigued with the potential fun of restoring a quite ancient car, I pondered the possibilities of such a venture. Final arrangements to pay for and go get it were made. Getting it turned out to be a whopper of a job. By then, in late 1957 or '58, John was in high school, and Dan was preparing to enlist in the U. S. Air Force, and Jim was 10-ish, too young to be much of a mechanic.

On a stormy Western Oregon November Sunday morning, Dan and I took off in the big Cascade company flatbed truck which was equipped with a power winch for loading machinery. The Buick, we learned, had been parked for 27 years in a remote, dilapidated, roofless shed, a long half-mile off a gravel country road. One of my employees was aware of our trip to get the car, without my knowing of his interest in the project, appeared on the scene just at the critical time to help as we were attempting to load the tired-out old touring car. Good fortune smiled on us additionally because by the time we were ready to move away from the loading point, rain was coming down relentlessly. Slipping and sliding, we barely made it back to the gravel road.

We arrived in McMinnville long after dark, tired and wet. We parked the loaded truck, with its decrepit cargo, in our driveway. Next morning, when Wendy surveyed what we had brought home from our exhaustive trip, she was appalled. As I look back 40 years, as this is written, and recall what was involved in that venture, it now seems even more monumental.

Our 1918 Model E Buick 7-passenger touring car

The model E Big Six Buick engine came to life for the first time in 27 years, with much coaxing and cranking via a heavy-duty electric shop drill and copious cans of ether starting-fluid. Refurbished with new upholstery, new floor panels and running boards, a new black canvas top on the original bows, a midnight blue body paint job with black fenders, splash aprons and radiator shell, and new set of lifetime tires, the old car was ready to run on short trips.

The ancient Buick, resplendent with new paint job and canvas top, commanded considerable attention in the country town of McMinnville. Small family outings complete with a basket lunch, local parades and special "showings" made for good fun as the old model E6 strutted noisily here and there. Later, when our family would move to Southern California, our plans wouldn't include the somewhat noble Buick. Though shod with new tires, it just was not capable of either being towed or driven those 1100 miles to a new home in Glendora. Reluctantly, prior to moving day in January 1963, I was obliged, with some trepidation, to find a buyer for my fond relic. The new buyer eagerly took over, ending my tryst with the handsome E6.

In the years of 1957 and 1958, as the U. S. economy struggled with a larger than "mini" recession, small businesses had their problems. We floundered some, carrying on the business, trying to make profitable sales, stay in the black and maintain an acceptable relationship with our local banker. After three years, with some halting, but mostly steady improvement of the business climate, our little Yamhill County world seemed to turn quite well on its Western Oregon axis.

Nearly three years later, however, with the two older boys enlisted in the Air Force, our local family of four chose to sell, re-buy and move to a brand new smaller three-bedroom little gem bungalow on West 22nd in McMinnville. With a nice patio and outdoor "barbe," new lawns and shrubs, and the addition of a cozy family room, it was just right.

Business-wise, interesting events began occurring. The general tractor and implement end was showing improvement. Competition caused by a John Deere company-owned store in Salem, a short 22 miles away, caused much anxiety and problems. My objections to JD management in Portland brought me nothing but more headaches.

The Columbus Day hurricane hit Western Oregon full force with 125 mph winds and torrential rains recorded in Portland, Oregon. At precisely 4:30 p.m., at the storm's height, I was landing at the Portland International Airport from a business trip in the roughest approach a Boeing 720B aircraft had ever made. Wendy and Mary Ann had picked their perilous way in to the terminal from McMinnville to meet me. Once on the ground and secured, we disembarked into the worst wind and rain storm ever recorded there.

Our trip home, as dusk settled, was most unstable and scary with power lines and trees down everywhere in our path. Yamhill County was devastated, and completely dark with no power or phones. Our new home was one of a select few that withstood the fury with no damage. Jim, at 14, had stayed home, in our backyard shooting baskets with friend Jeb Bladine, until the wind robbed them of the ball during a quick jump shot. The Columbus Day Storm lingers, through all the years, as our family's most frightful weather experience. Mary Ann particularly was shaken measurably by the frightening general destruction.

Our family experience in McMinnville for nearly six years was rewarding, eventful and challenging. Many lasting friendships accrued. The children grew. Both Daniel and John joined the Air Force for extended periods of duty. Mary Ann and Jim led happy lives as they grew toward the teenage years.

At this juncture in my memoirs, I now turn to "The Long Winding Trail ~ The Career Years" detailing the business world that unfolded for me.

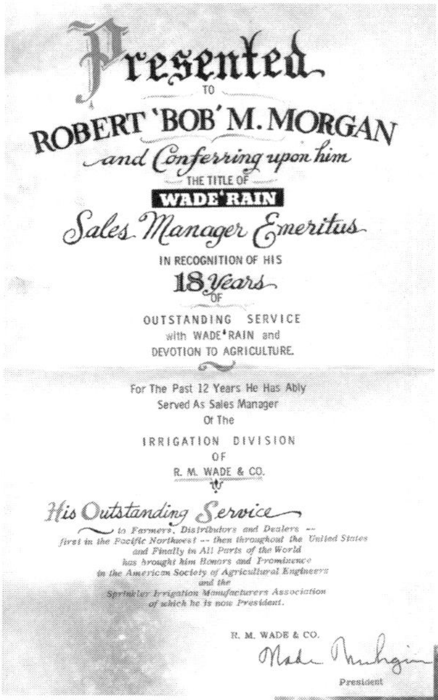
Presented
TO
ROBERT 'BOB' M. MORGAN
and Conferring upon him
THE TITLE OF
WADE RAIN
Sales Manager Emeritus
IN RECOGNITION OF HIS
18 Years
OF
OUTSTANDING SERVICE
with WADE RAIN and
DEVOTION TO AGRICULTURE.

For The Past 12 Years He Has Ably
Served As Sales Manager
Of The
IRRIGATION DIVISION
OF
R. M. WADE & CO.

His Outstanding Service
to Farmers, Distributors and Dealers --
first in the Pacific Northwest -- then throughout the United States
and Finally in All Parts of the World
has brought him Honors and Prominence
in the American Society of Agricultural Engineers
and the
Sprinkler Irrigation Manufacturers Association
of which he is now President.

R. M. WADE & CO.
President

Sales Manager Certificate from Wade Rain

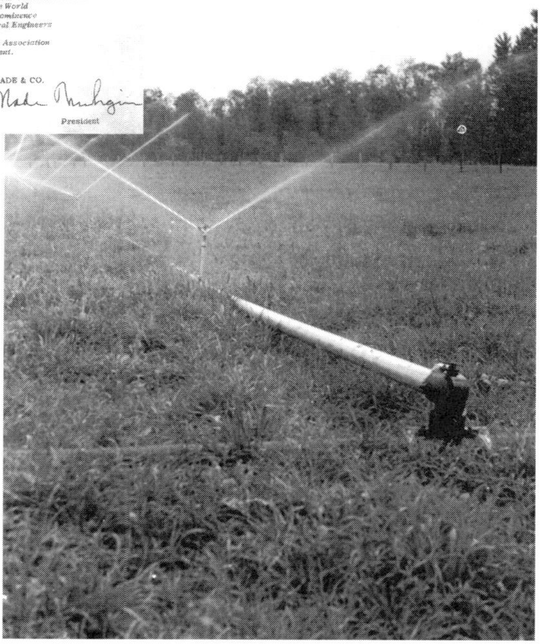

Original version of a Wade Rain overhead portable sprinkler irrigation system

PART THREE

THE LONG WINDING TRAIL ~ THE CAREER YEARS

*T*he electrifying news that World War II had ended caused massive activities in the national business community as U. S. organizations hustled to gain a competitive position in the mainstream of private enterprise. My employer, R. M. Wade & Co., was prepared to quickly direct all efforts toward modernizing the crude Wade Rain portable sprinkler irrigation equipment it had made prior to 1941 and target itself as a leader in the American irrigation industry.

After complete re-tooling, Wade Manufacturing, the production division, soon developed a new light-weight steel quick-coupler. It was attached to newly available aluminum tubing to make up portable overhead sprinkler irrigation systems. The short-comings and several changes and modifications, inherent in new product design, were unfortunately prevalent in the new Wade Rain quick coupler. The problem couplers and companion fittings were inadvertently shipped all over the United States to newly appointed Wade Rain distributors who were immediately disturbed and often angry as they tried to make the equipment function. It was in that company-defensive atmosphere that I was appointed National Wade Rain Sales Manager in late 1945.

Robert M. Morgan, National Sales Manager for Wade Rain

Six years into marriage and the father of three, I pinched myself, reflecting on my country background and suddenly being thrust into a position of responsibility in a continental business environment that included searing demands. My Sales Manager job description included setting up Wade Rain dealers in the Northwestern states and distributors elsewhere in the United States, Canada and Mexico, arranging promotions such as sales meetings and initiating advertising programs.

Our factory portable sprinkler irrigation equipment

problems brought on almost daily meetings and countless trips to the Wade Manufacturing plant located in northwest Portland's Mock's Bottom, just off old Highway 30, the St. Helens road. Seemingly endless periods on the long distance telephone, pacifying and reassuring customers of prompt product corrections, dispatched by airfreight, were the "order of my days" from 6:00 a.m. to long after office hours, week in and week out. By 1948, our product line had improved, resulting in public acceptance which dramatically increased our volume of sales.

My association with Adolph Bloch Advertising Agency, which handled all of Wade's promotion in those super busy, sometimes hectic, yet exciting years, was a rewarding aspect that brought much joy and valuable experience to me. "Ad," as Adolph Bloch was known in the trade, had represented Wade & Co. for years. He was of Jewish extraction and was an extra-hard-working, jovial, super honest perfectionist who plied his trade with aplomb and straight-line accuracy. Although my senior by several years, we became fine friends both on the fast track and in the relaxed comfort of our respective homes.

Memorable luncheons at the Club of which Ad was a member, after a jam-packed morning's work, are still standouts. Ad's gracious wife Edna was, for many years, recognized as one of Portland's ten best dressed woman. Ad's warm friendship was a non-registered perquisite to my job that had a many-fold meaning as my business life took shape.

Five years following World War II, in 1950, aluminum tubing, of which Wade used many carloads, had become plentiful and portable. Sprinkler irrigation was high on the list of agricultural benefits to American farmers. Wade Rain was popular, and production and sales grew rapidly. Within a year, the United States became embroiled in the

Korean war. Again, as in World War II, demand on national resources for the war effort took precedence over civilian use, necessitating a concerted effort to obtain priorities to make aluminum available as an essential element for irrigation in the production of food and fiber.

I made many trips to Washington DC attendant with our appeals to the war Production Board for aluminum tonnage allocations. Finally a constant irrigation industry presence in the capitol was deemed imperative. R. M. Wade & Co. loaned one of my salesmen, Robert C. Mueller, to the industry, acting as an on-site emissary to promote civilian use of aluminum for irrigation.

That Washington experience prepared Bob Mueller to later become our trade association Executive Secretary directing the activities of the Irrigation Association from a Washington DC office, a position he held for several years.

One of Wade's former salesmen, employed before I became involved, Hobart William Stout, inventor and entrepreneur, was credited with building a new device described as a wheeled side-roll aluminum sprinkler lateral pipe-line in 1947.

Wade recognized the potential for a side-roll lateral for sprinkler irrigation and by 1951 was prepared to manufacture our version named Wade Rain Power-Roll. It was powered by a portable gas engine drive unit. We introduced the Power-Roll with great fanfare at our annual Wade Rain sales meeting in February 1952. With an impressive display on Multnomah Stadium field, the Power-Roll was laid out below the spacious veranda of the Multnomah Athletic Club. Over one hundred Wade Rain dealers were assembled to view the demonstration panorama.

It took a lot of preparation for that sales meeting of which I was in charge. So enthusiastic was the dealer acceptance, Wade Rain Power-Roll quickly became a leader and still is after 45 years. Much sprinkler irrigation expansion took place in the ensuing years as my pace seemed to ever quicken, traveling almost constantly to promote the Wade Rain name. The pressure was always on for more volume. New territories in foreign countries beckoned as we grew.

My first international connection unfolded when we contracted with Irrigation Development Corporation of New York City as the Wade Rain agent representing us in some seventeen countries, including those in South America. IDC was an offshoot of a tobacco importing group of Belgian-Jewish refugees that settled in New York City about 1939 after having escaped the ravages of the Hitler regime.

The founder's nephew, Andrew Gilbert, and an associate, Mark Hamilton, both also pre-War II Jewish refugees, were the principals of IDC. My many trips to New York to work with them resulted in a close personal relationship having developed with them and their wives.

With proper IDC advanced introductions, one significant foreign trip I made was to the South American Countries of Columbia, Peru and Brazil, with stops at the Central American cities of Guatemala City, San Salvador, Managua and Panama City in 1953 to introduce Wade Rain sprinkler irrigation. Each of those countries desperately needed the advantages of efficient overhead irrigation. These were gratifying and fruitful experiences, meeting new important people in far away places and applying new design irrigation equipment to centuries-old crops in the Americas such as Brazil's coffee in the state of Parana. Living in and exploring Brazil's principal cities of Rio de Janeiro, Sao Paulo and the port city of Santos were memorable side-lights to a country boy.

Radial piston engines still propelled all commercial aircraft in 1953, including the Boeing DC6s and Lockheed Constellations, the long-haul rugged planes most used then, even though they each had certain limitations. The air-leg from Lima, Peru, to Rio de Janeiro was significant in that the heights of the Andes mountains dictated minimum flight altitudes of 30,000 feet, which required over-flying the summits no later than 1:00 p.m. daily, due to the high-level storm systems created by daily heat inversions. As we prepared to depart Lima, mechanical problems delayed departures two days in a row because we could not start early enough to meet the 1:00 p.m. mountain summit deadlines. Two lost days meant phone calls to people I didn't know, to change schedules and reservations.

The La Paz, Bolivia, commercial airport runway was listed as 21,000 feet above sea-level, highest in the world, quite a revelation to a swamp land rover such as I. The return to the states on that trip with stops at Belim, Brazil at the mouth of the Amazon River, Caracas, Venezuela, Curacao, Port-au-Prince, then back to Miami was significant, as I visited so many strange points for irrigation.

Wendy, dear heart, mothered the family and tended the farm with son Dan's help as I was rarely home except for selected week-ends when there was always much to do. By 1953, our farm home was comfortable with a concrete-floored full basement and garage, a new oil-fired furnace, plus a nicely done outdoor yellow paint job, plus two sides with a full width, riverfront and south-side concrete patio. Life on the farm was becoming inviting.

Other standout trips were several to Mexico to set up a Wade Rain distributorship with Francisco J. Jimeno and his Equipos Y Accessorios of Mexico City. The long-standing friendship with Francisco, affectionately known in business as "Paco," continues to this day. Paco's industrious efforts in introducing portable overhead sprinkler irrigation to his native country have brought him great public acclaim there.

Although Australia had produced some imitations of U. S. or English agricultural sprinkler heads, the people down-under knew very little about quick-coupling, overhead sprinkler irrigation. Our international Wade Rain agents, IDC of New York, informed us of the impressive potential for sale of Wade Rain in the new Australia agricultural market. Talks and correspondence with Howard Rotovator Ltd. of Sidney soon established a format for plans to make direct contact down-under and get our product, Wade Rain in use in the substantial farm lands of Eastern Australia from Brisbane south to Melbourne.

With much preparation and advanced shipments of equipment for me to demonstrate during my carefully planned and rather lengthy stay in Australia, I left Portland in early October for a most eventful and educational experience with the Howard Rotorvator people and their chief engineer in particular, Perc Thomas, my guide and host there.

In 1953 organized air transportation worldwide was the norm. On that certain early October day, after having carefully gone over all family and farm matters with Wendy and son Daniel, who was by then 14 years old, I flew out of Portland. The first stop was to San Francisco for overseas connections with Untied Airlines service to Hawaii. There I spent several days with the Honolulu Iron Works people surveying irrigation projects on Oahu, Molakai and the pineapple growing island of Lanai.

Departing Honolulu by Qantas Airlines in those propeller-driven days, the South Seas air route was via a refueling stop 1600 mile south of Pearl Harbor on Canton

Island, a coral reef with an adequate landing strip for trans-pacific planes. The island itself was and is today barely identified on most maps of the Pacific Ocean. From Canton Island, the next air-leg was Fiji Island. After refueling, Sidney, Australia, 1200 miles to the southwest, was the final destination.

With much newspaper coverage and many public meetings, plus extensive traveling along the east coast of Australia, portable overhead sprinkler irrigation quickly became better known in that land which was then at least 20 years behind the U.S. in many technical fields. *The Land newspaper, LTD,* of Sidney ran a banner headline, "Irrigation -U. S. Expert Sees Big Potential." After several weeks of intense effort in the introduction of our latest U. S. knowledge concerning overhead sprinkler irrigation, I departed the lovable land of Australia and my new business acquaintances. The experience of meeting the indefatigable Ausies, learning their searching desire to figure out all they could about Americans and their somewhat parallel, but strikingly different, ways, sayings and accomplishments, was quite an education for all of us.

Although troublesome at the time, the only glitch in the return trip from Australia occurred as our PanAmerican World Airways Strato-Cruiser approached the Oregon coast and final touchdown at Portland International Airport. In preparation for the final approach and landing, the aircraft nose-wheel gear failed to let down. With a flurry of activity, the flight engineer scurried down from the flight deck to the lower deck, through a forward bulk-head hatchway and manually cranked down the nose-wheel into position for landing. This succession of movements, however, caused us to fly-by and circle around to align the aircraft for the final approach and uneventful landing at Portland.

Arriving home, I received a warm family welcome to find things quite normal on our Sauvie Island farm. Thanks to my darling wife Lucy and her all-encompassing capacity as mother and ranch manager.

The years through 1954 and beyond rapidly went by as the pressure pace at R. M. Wade & Co. mounted and overhead sprinkler irrigation took on new prominence with advancements in design, including side-wheel roll, the introduction of labor-saving Center Pivot systems which caught the fancy of big area irrigators. Solid-set sprinkler designs also opened vistas for semi-automatic irrigation on high value cash crops such as cotton, citrus, lettuce, tomatoes and potatoes.

By 1956 my successes in sales, the comparatively smooth farm operation and the pressure-cooker demands of the National Wade Rain Sales Manager's job raised signals in my mind about the values of life, the fast track I was on and just how I should plan my family's future.

A former Wade co-worker, Cliff Cornutt, had left Wade ten years previously, buying into the John Deere dealership in Hillsboro, Oregon. His successes were noteworthy there to the extent that he and his partner Roy Hofer had purchased the John Deere dealership, Cascade Tractor and Implement Company in neighboring McMinnville, thirty miles to the southwest. The Cascade absentee-ownership had not gone well. Cornutt and Hofer were looking for a part owner-manager to take over and coordinate with their management style.

The more I talked with Cliff about Cascade, the more interested I became in the possibilities of having an ownership interest in my own business and the adventure of settling down in the quietude of a small country town that could also be a fine setting for our children's best interests. As 1957 was ushered in, I seriously made plans for a big change. I secured an arrangement with Cornutt and Hofer to buy a third-interest in Cascade for $25,000.00 cash. I put the farm up for sale and subsequently gave Wade notice to leave.

After having purchased a home in McMinnville on 13th and Thompson Lane, the big move took place on June 15, 1957, even though the farm had not yet been sold. We settled in and I took over as a part owner of Cascade Tractor and Implement Company.

It was a totally new experience and a business fraught with the average number of operational problems, although the staff of employees was very experienced and capable, needing only top-notch managerial guidance, which I found I lacked expertise in.

The Cascade/John Deere dealership was long-standing and well established. Competition from neighboring JD dealers was just one of many problems I had not reckoned with in my early planning.

Life in McMinnville was a completely pleasant experience for our entire family. My college friends and fraternity brothers, Jim Stanard, then vice-president of the First National Bank, and Weldon Ross, a leading doctor, all extended themselves to make us welcome and part of the community.

1957 developed as one of the more serious recession years for our national economy and it quickly became apparent to me that Cascade and I were in the middle of a depressed period. My staff made note of how good business had been the first five years following World War II, by comparison with the second five year period up to 1955, two years before my arrival. I rapidly learned the downside of operating a business in a tightly-knit community where all of the established farmers were either related, grew up together or owed each other money or favors.

Keeping a level cash flow, meeting Friday payrolls, satisfying the John Deere Plow Company, maintaining an aging physical plant and meeting or beating competition abruptly focused my business gaze on the seriousness of making a small operation show a profit with very limited operating capital. The excitement of concluding a substantial sale and the satisfaction of an acceptable balance sheet were my exhilaration and challenge that made Cascade attractive.

At 45 years of age, however, after having been a Sales Manager of an international organization for ten years, traveling the high road, with a wide selection of contacts, meeting important people daily and seeing new and exciting facets of business unfold, perhaps, had made a mark on me, causing me to wonder if, after my change to the more subdued life, I might be missing a lot of the world as it went by.

A highlight during my years with Cascade was my fortunate discussion one day with Glenn Christianson, one of Yamhill County's best farmers. Among other crops, Glenn annually grew about 50 acres of Crimson clover as a seed crop. Crimson clover was an early maturing plant that was always difficult to thresh with a conventional, rasp-bar-cylinder combine. Being a very meticulous operator, Glenn searched for a means of threshing Crimson clover with a minimum of seed damage. He had come to the conclusion that soft-rubber fillers in about 50 percent of the open spaces of the combine cylinder concave grate would perhaps provide a softer surface for the cylinder rasp-bars to rub the clover seed hulls against, eliminating crackage, thereby producing a higher germination test seed.

After lengthy discussions with Glenn on the subject, I one day asked him if he would like to join me in making some test-trial rubberized bars to try during the next harvest season. He said he couldn't support me financially, but would help otherwise, any way he could.

Going at making the first test rubberized concave bars alone, I found them to be very effective and soon, as the word spread, many farmers bought what soon came to be known as MORGAN RUBBER CONCAVE BARS, for raspbar combine harvesters. We made the bars at Cascade as a "shop" production item, billing them to local farmers as a Cascade combine attachment.

Profits were good and within a year I formed R. M. Morgan Co. with three other investors and, as a manufacturer, sold and distributed the bars nationally. The proceeds from that venture were alluring to the extent that my interest in Cascade was diluted. I began to contemplate ways of divesting myself of the farm equipment dealership.

In 1962, while traveling in southern California in the interest of Morgan Rubber Bars, I received a phone call from my long-time friend, Crawford Reid, suggesting that his employer, Rainbird Sprinkler Manufacturing Corp., was planning to hire a sales assistant for him. He informed me, that if I were interested, that I should plan to come to Glendora at the earliest time to talk with Clem and Betty La Fetra, the owners.

I immediately called home, discussing with Wendy this dramatic turn of events and the potential for a great opportunity. With a favorable feeling to the possibility of making another big business and family change, I hastily went to Rainbird's office in Glendora. The discussions were favorable and, shortly thereafter, I made tracks for home that October day with a promise of a national assistant sales manager's job in my pocket, dependent on my satisfactorily resolving my responsibilities at Cascade and

Morgan Co. This all appears to have been done quite easily with the La Fetras. The facts were that we had long since developed an easy rapport through the years, both Clem and Betty LaFetra were exceptionally affable, understanding, progressive friends.

I was able to quickly sell my interest in Cascade back to my partners, Cliff Cornutt and Roy Hofer, at no profit. I was also able to operate Morgan Co. remotely, thanks to fine cooperation from my associates in that enterprise.

Confirming my acceptance of Rainbird's offer of employment, I went on their payroll October 15, 1962, spending some indoctrination times at the factory in November. We subsequently prepared to sell our McMinnville home on West 22nd Street. Although it was a new, very livable home with lots of extras, the market was slow, and we were obliged to carry it for a whole year before selling it at no profit.

By January 25, 1963, the Morgan family prepared to move to Southern California. We took up residence in a fine seven-year-old house at 521 W. Richardson Lane in Glendora that had been home to Betty LaFetra's mother prior to her recent death the previous October. At a most nominal rent, Betty suggested we live there for a year, looking around at other potential homes in the interim and if we concluded, which we did after one year, that we would like to buy her home, she would apply all rental money paid toward a most favorable purchase price of a total of $37,500.00.

The big change had been accomplished, but now our family was somewhat fragmented. Mary Ann stayed in McMinnville to attend Linfield College. Jim enrolled at Glendora High School to complete his freshman year. John, then in the Air Force at nearby Edwards Air Force Base in the Mojave desert, was able to come to our new

Glendora home regularly. Dan, by then three years in the Air Force, was stationed in Reykjevik, Iceland, flying the Early Dew Line as a Douglas C46 flight mechanic.

That January also marked other family changes. My father died on January 9th at age 76, following a prolonged illness. It brought sadness to all , but particularly for Margaret Matilda Schuler Morgan, a steadfast, loving wife to Newton for 26 years following their marriage in 1937. They had spent those happy years living variously in California and Oregon. Kind and proper lady that she was, she was cast adrift with Dad's passing. I had been with them briefly two days before Dad died.

The family was all signaled at once when father Newton died. We were in McMinnville, closing out our business and home there preparatory to moving. John, youthful U. S. Airman that he was, jumped in to breach the family loss. Rushing to Hemet, California from Edwards Air Force Base, he helped Grandmother Margaret in every way, taking full charge with the funeral and burial arrangements. Following those final rites at Hemet, John saw Grandmother on the train to Portland where we picked her up to come live with us briefly prior to our exodus there and our move to California. This effort by John signaled fine, loving maturity on his part at a trying time.

Following our resettling in the new surroundings of Glendora on January 26th. 1963, the days vanished into months which, in turn, were transformed into years as time scudded by. It was a happy, upscale time as we all became our individual parts of a new and different, fast-moving world of excitement and challenges considerably beyond the lower key of Webfoot living.

After a year at Linfield, Mary Ann came home to Glendora, embarking on a work ethic that expanded her capabilities from a neophyte in business, through the years, to an accomplished executive secretary in an elevated environment.

John finished his assigned stint in the Air Force, moving also to Glendora, soon getting into the civilian work world and eventual marriage to Danielle Lavine. Their busy lives, as their family grew to include two daughters and a son, took them from Southern California to Portland, Oregon, to Rockford, Illinois, then on to Houston, Texas, to Colorado Springs, Colorado, and finally, full circle back to California's Simi Valley. They were divorced after 16 years of marriage.

James graduated from Glendora High School after enjoying many pleasurable teen years. He worked at various jobs for a period, and then joined the United States Marine Corps. He served admirably in Vietnam for a full hitch before returning to civilian status in Southern California for a short four years before marrying Ann Nuenschwander in 1969.

The years with Rain Bird were full and exciting as the Company expanded rapidly in a new and different atmosphere with son Anthony LaFetra having graduated from Stanford University and in the process, bringing into Rain Bird a new breed of junior executive friends of his, all attuned to hi-tech business styles not akin to the grass-roots, home-spun, family approach that had made his father Clem and Mother Betty so exceedingly successful with RainBird sprinklers through the previous three decades.

Clement LaFetra, due to a heart condition, would leave this world much too young, dying two days before John Kennedy was assassinated. The combination of Clem's affable nature and his understanding of values, coupled with his wife Betty's highly practical business capabilities, made a team that brought the simple 1934 beginning of Rain Bird to a strikingly successful business in the following thirty years.

My long time friend Crawford Reid, godfather to the LaFetra children and National Sales Manager of RainBird, and I seemed to fit perfectly in advancing the sales programs of RainBird. By 1966, Crawford was ready to retire. The LaFetras' son Anthony and his high-tech junior executive friends were, in Clem's absence, taking RainBird along a sophisticated, elevated course that was obviously not going to include me at age 54. Some 25 years their senior and with only minor college credentials to vie with their abundance of Stanford degrees, it appeared my days at RainBird were numbered. It was time for me to re-align myself elsewhere.

During the RainBird years, we had established a farm equipment distributorship known as Foothill Sales, representing Portable Elevator Mfg. Co. of Bloomington, Illinois and Bush Hog Inc. of Selma, Alabama, both very fine lines, new in the southwest states. At my departure from RainBird, Portable Elevator offered me an Assistant Sales Manager's position at their factory. Moving my family to Bloomington proved to be totally unacceptable to us Westerners, and I was shortly obliged to withdraw from the Portable offer. W. A. Matheson, Sr., Portable's President and fine friend that he was, then offered to appoint me as Portable's factory agent, operating only on a sales commission in the states of California and Arizona. It was an offer that I readily accepted, and one that subsequently provided me with a good living and an avenue for other opportunities. A few years as a Manufacturer's Representative served me well until Portable's powerful Canadian Distributor chose to open a Western distributorship, insisting that California and Arizona be included, which canceled me out. I again found myself at a crossroads, but not for long.

While attending the Farm Equipment Manufacturers Association meeting in Denver, I was approached by an agent for Melnor Industries of Moonachie, New Jersey. As national distributors and manufacturers of irrigation, he advised that Melnor was considering getting into the irrigation industry with a line of sprinklers manufactured in Israel. A working arrangement was soon effected, and I went on Melnor's payroll as a Vice President, National Agricultural Sprinkler Sales.

With yet another beginning, I embarked on a vigorous and wide-ranging program to get Israeli sprinklers accepted in the United States, and ultimately generate sales that would keep Melnor, a four billion dollar sales division of Beatrice Foods, Inc. of Chicago, interested in advancing in a field they knew nothing about. After a great expenditure by Melnor and a massive effort on my part, it became obvious that Israeli sprinkler heads would never displace RainBird and Buckner, two historically fine agricultural sprinkler lines.

The Melnor bubble burst for me about 1973. Because I had been warehousing the Melnor products in rented property in Covina, California, belonging to Jerry Edgar, a business man with many interests, I embarked on what ultimately would be one of my most profitable business experiences. Jerry and I were soon well acquainted and, as time went by, investment opportunities surfaced. One day, Jerry suggested that we consider buying a business building in downtown Covina that was for sale for $55,000.00. It developed that, as partners, we could finance it (on a 50%-50% basis) for $10,000.00 down and $800.00 monthly bank contract payments. The building's commercial renters provided a monthly gross revenue sufficient to cover all costs of taxes, insurance and maintenance. Jerry and I shortly concluded that the two-story, 70-year-old building was justifiably acquirable. The purchase in 1973 turned out to be a very attractive investment.

Fifteen years later, after having received an annual net income, before taxes, of $3,000.00 to $4,000.00, and with our bank contract having been paid down to less than $3,000.00, we agreed to put the building up for sale at the peak of the Southern California real estate boom in 1988. Within weeks, our agent came up with a buyer who agreed to our price of $325,000.00, with 20% down and monthly payments of interest only, of $2,000.00, all payments being equally divided between Edgar and me, an asset that has since served Jerry, who died in 1991, his estate and me these several years.

In 1976, at age 63, I still had a vigorous urge to have an active part in the irrigation industry and was alerted about May of that year by my good friend Bill Henderickson that The Toro Company, irrigation sprinkler manufacturer, was interested in getting into the agricultural sprinkler market with a modified version of its successful gear-driven turf sprinkler heads. I went on board with Toro on July 1, 1976, to lead a fast, but exciting and rewarding several years, as the American economy was on one of its most progressive upswings.

The "TORO WORLD" was an upscale, very administrative, executive-driven corporate structure of nice guys often over-powered with headquarters initiatives that too frequently caused them to come up short on the balance sheet. Personnel-wise, I never worked with finer people, many of whom became lasting friends. It was with Toro that I got my best broadside view of how a Fortune-500 company of comparatively modest size functions.

In 1980, as the U. S. economy faltered and Toro's fortunes dipped to frighteningly low levels, my experience there ended with some heart-felt goodbyes. I knew that, at age 67, the executive work force legions were diminishing for me with each new day. Not being convinced that there was a stopping point in my business activities, August 1, 1980, found me back in the saddle with an unknown company labeled I³ (International-

Robert M. Morgan's Engineering Certificate

Irrigation-Industries), directly administered to by a large successful national aerospace company with headquarters in Alabama.

My introduction to I³ came about as a result of a firm friendship of several years with my good acquaintance Eddy Beem, an Israeli who traveled worldwide for Peleg of Tel Aviv, Israel, selling the very same agricultural sprinklers I had been unable to promote for Melnor Industries. Eddy Beem had convinced Richard Rasmaussen, Northridge, California's manager of floundering I³, that Peleg sprinkler heads could compete in America with RainBird, Buckner and Toro. Great effort was expended for several years, but it was not in the marketing cards to break into such a selective field with Peleg's questionable quality.

Another Israeli product line that had not been explored at all by I³ was the unique Inbal hydraulic valve, also available to I³. It was a very salable product that took off quite well, but was eventually put in the background when Rasmussen, with heavy pressure from the headquarters parent company, negotiated and sold I³ to a South African company.

Further individual sales efforts with industry friends finally led to an end of my active selling career in 1986. My working goal, after having arrived at age 71.5 years, when Social Security payments were scheduled to begin, drew to a close in 1983 and soon thereafter I embarked on full-time retirement. Recurring deposits in and adjustments to the near record high Social Security allowance I had earned through the years left me with a comfortable base.

I could never have imagined such an illustrious and gratifying business life when my one-and-only Lucy Ann and I were married at ages 25, as we embarked on our once-in-a-lifetime marital voyage which continues, as always as this chapter is written, approaching 60 years.

THROUGH THE ROOF

During the Melnor years, by some happenstance, I became acquainted with a man who had applied for a patent for a most unusual, large-area-of-coverage, pop-up sprinkler that incorporated use of an air-pressure tank that accumulated a modestly high water pressure, timed so that it exhausted about two gallons of pressurized water through a large nozzle to achieve a great distance-of-throw. While discharging water, it also popped up and by an indexing quadrant moved three degrees of a circle. Having completed the cycle, it repeated the movement a total of six times per minute.

The entire principle was very intriguing to a lot of potential users. I made up a dozen all-metal sprinklers, using a small conventional steel pressure tank. With a demonstration plot at Cal Poly Pomona's AG Engineering Lab, excitement for the sprinkler concept expanded rapidly. Through an industry friend, Bob Tait in British Columbia, we made an installation on a B. C. golf course fairway with excellent reception. Bob Tait was a good salesman and soon had tentative orders from several golf clubs for enough sprinklers to cover 18 fairways.

Meanwhile, I promoted the sprinkler, naming it L.A.R. (Low-Application-Rate), introducing it to Melnor to the extent that they chose to duplicate my all-metal model in a plastic version in their factory engineering department. After much design effort, the day finally came to make the first test of their plastic counterpart to the metal L.A.R. Using normal city water pressure, they turned it on in the lab.

I had not been present during any of the Melnor reconstruction of L.A.R. in their lab. The first surge of water through L.A.R., at standard city pressure, created a combustion in the plastic counterparts of proportions beyond any calculations of Melnor's Engineering Department. An explosion occurred that blew the entire contraption, vertically, through the factory shop roof. Such a confounding miscalculation and resultant calamity foretold an immediate cancellation of any further experimentation. L.A.R.'s death-knell resounded with reverberations that ended my Melnor association.

Robert and Lucy Ann Morgan
at their 50th Wedding Anniversary
December, 1988

PART FOUR

REFLECTIONS ~ HAPPENINGS GREAT AND SMALL

It must be recorded that these happenings are my impressions of over half a century with a wonderful person, always a lady, always loving, forever upbeat, permanently happy and graced with an everlasting smile. Her impressions would have much more polish than mine, and be more detailed, always in her nice way.

It has been a "Garden of Memories" which I now reflect upon as the harvest of so many years. These are rewards for which I remain forever grateful.

Retirement too has had its rewards. Twelve-hour to fourteen-hour work days quickly dissolve into the past. Missed, though, is the excitement of each new morning as another inning of the endless "Ball Game" challenged one's effectiveness.

The quietness of a secure, regulated life stands in contrast to the business world's other side of madding crowds, curt commands from office headquarters and clients' crisp edicts.

The uneasy waits in air terminals for flight departures, extending from "on time," to three-day delays had their tedious effects on business appointments at the other ends of planned schedules. In retirement 8:00 a.m. deadlines have faded into oblivion.

Now those hours have arrived when there are no more concerns for Lucy and me as to how to meet the household needs. These times are blessed with that wonderful storehouse of life-long friends and relatives, the pleasant daily requirements of caring for one another and making an always foremost effort to serve the will of God.

With nearly sixty years of marriage our hallmark, I look with pride upon Lucy's and my long tenure together. She has unceasingly been the most wonderful wife and homemaker of inestimable style. With that never-ending smile, she cheerfully endured those "Ten Thousand Goodbyes."

After all of these pages, this is a story of my life. As I approach the end of these writings, it occurs that I can best make complimentary and endearing comments about family members who participated to one extent or another in my varied endeavors through the years.

Favorite articles reprinted with permission from *The Sauvie Island Outlook* are related here as cherished memories that aptly illustrate our heritage. Random reflections, seemingly revisited from the timeline of earlier chapters, deserve comment better served by perspective. Poignant letters and tributes in rhyme are re-printed here, too, as part of our collective legacy.

Our family structure, knitted with progeny, added to our clan in each family segment. What started as just Lucy Ann and me has burgeoned into a combined grouping of children, grandchildren, great grandchildren and in-laws, rounding out to twenty.

We have prospered the past 25 years as a complex world has portioned goodness and prosperity to all of us in accordance with our receptiveness and trust.

Wendy and I have certainly enjoyed not only the myriad family good times, but also the advantages of a host of American travel trips mostly related to my executive status in business and our long allegiance to my business trade-group, the Irrigation Association.

Then there have been our great trips in many parts of the world. Not many home-makers have made ten Atlantic crossings as has Wendy. Also the great Canadian, Hawaiian, Mexican and Alaskan adventures are always to be remembered.

The ultimate honor to our original matrimonial vows was unquestionably our 50th Wedding Anniversary, so expertly and lavishly accomplished by the deft prowess of our Mary Ann, John, James and their families, December 10, 1988.

Following the celebration of our 50th, our English family of Jennifer, David, Nicholas and Emma Baker stayed with us for nearly four weeks, returning home in late December. Wendy and I immediately jumped into our next big move. We had sold our Glendora home of 26 years, purchased a smaller abode at Champagne Village in Escondido, California, together with the acquisition of our new Oregon summer home at Salishan, Gleneden Beach,

Lincoln County.

The exertion of such great change aside, our new lifestyle turned out to be most comfortable and rewarding. As this seemingly long accounting draws ever-closer to a conclusion, there is still more to be recorded about a largely average life, blessed abundantly by the many souls that came my way, starting that certain hour March 3, 1913.

As we look back through the decades, some of our earliest family fun times were vacationing on the Oregon Coast, sometimes at Nelscott, now part of Lincoln City, a spot within two shoreline miles north of our present-day home at Salishan, Gleneden Beach. Then, with only two boys in our earliest years, we couldn't have imagined that nearly half a century later we would have such a beautiful and prestigious full-time home at Salishan Seaview, Inc.

In 1968, Lucy's evangelistic research caused her to renounce her considerable relationship of nearly 40 years with the Christian Science Church in order that she might earnestly follow selected Bible teachings. It was then, with good guidance, that she sought and discovered the full meanings of God's scriptural words. Then, in consort, after some visitations, we became members of Bethany Baptist Church of West Covina.

The fine friends, soon discovered, together with the good old ones such as the transplanted Cliff Burkes of an earlier Oregon era, Miles and Mabel Thomas, Miles being Dad's cousin, my Alpha Tau Omega brother John Kehrli and wife Georgia, plus the comings and goings of my cousins June and husband Bill Tillman, as well as Scott and Anita Copeland. They all became a part of our intensely busy California lives.

Again new friendships and a quickly blossoming closeness with Pastor Lloyd T. Anderson and his wife

Marion brought us many invigorating times that included a Holy Lands tour in August 1969 that generated never-to-be-forgotten memories.

Upon returning home, our hearts and minds brimming with the exhilaration of such a trip were soon turned to sadness when our oldest son Daniel died in mid-September 1969, just shy of his 30th birthday, leaving behind his lovely British wife Jennifer and 18-month-old son Nicholas, our first grandchild.

Healings came slowly as we all attempted to patch the void created by Dan's passing. Jennie and Nicholas returned to Jennie's parents in Diss, England. Within a year, matrimony brought them a fine husband and father, David Baker, himself a young widower.

Many trips preceded and followed that mournful September 1969. Earlier, except for son John, who was then stationed at Edwards AFB, the family met with Dan in 1966, stationed at Andrews AFB, Washington D.C. Embarking on a grand eastern motoring tour, to Gettysburg, Jamestown, Williamsburg, New York City and Boston, we had a great family time before saying goodbye to Dan as he returned to Andrews. We headed west towards home, traveling 845 miles the last day.

A few years earlier, about 1965, the "Girls," Lucy Ann and Mary Ann, enjoyed a fine European trip with Dan while he was stationed at Weisbaden, Germany where they again motored, that time in Dan's Volkswagen traveling from Denmark through Germany to Austria, Switzerland, Italy, back to Switzerland, there leaving Dan who returned to duty in Germany. They then went by train to Paris, finally flying to London, little realizing that a few years later they would have English relatives a few miles to the north in Diss.

Briefly now, this memoir looks inside the lives of each

of our four children, in turn as they reached adulthood and produced families of their own.

Lucy Ann and our four children: John, Daniel, James and Mary Ann

DAN'S FAMILY

Dan and Jennifer's wedding

What had began as merely a fun evening of female fellowship for our yet-to-be daughter-in-law Jennifer Ann Wilby (born at Thetford, Norfolk in the United Kingdom on December 20, 1946) became much more. Seated in her car, while waiting momentarily for four girlfriends as the evening grew late, she fretted some about her dirty windshield. She emerged from her car and proceeded to brighten the glass. Unannounced, a tall young U. S. Airman stepped up, offering to not only clean her windshield, but to wipe the headlights, too. At that juncture, Jennifer's laughing friends bouncingly arrived. Daniel Munro Morgan, Sergeant First Class, was the airman. With certain aplomb, having demonstrated his cleaning ability, and without further introduction, eyed Jennifer seriously and asked if he could see her again one evening soon, without so many "gigglers" present.

Dan and Jennifer were married July 14, 1965, in St. Mary's Church at Diss, Norfolk, by Canon Corbell. Jennifer was of English heritage, and loved spending much of her childhood with her Grandfather, a farmer and veterinarian by trade. Her parents, Olive Francis Wilby and Ivan Philip Wilby (now deceased) provided her and her brother Stephen John Wilby (born October 10, 1950) with a comfortable home as they attended Diss schools. Later, Jennifer attended Norwich City College, where she studied

Food and Catering. Her deft abilities in that studied craft have made her a "mistress of nutrition" and a hostess unequaled as she plies the catering trade. Soon thereafter, engulfed in her catering talents, she became acquainted with David Ingram Baker (born September 17, 1939) and his wife Susan. Jennifer and Dan spent many happy evenings with their friends David and Susan Baker.

As the wife of a United States military man, English citizen Jennifer exulted somewhat at the future prospects of meeting Dan's western American family. The actuality of that meeting came more abruptly than she had any thought of. Dan's life-long physical limitations soon thereafter brought his hitch in the Air Force to an end. He was mustered out early in 1967. As a veteran, he and his English bride were transferred to Sacramento, California, with full benefits as he was treated at military hospitals.

By the spring of 1967, Jennifer and Dan were excitedly expecting their first-born. Although settled in Sacramento, Dan having medical care, holding a paying job and enrolled at Sacramento City College, they often made trips to our home in Glendora. At the proper, advanced time prior to Jennifer's impending delivery date, Lucy Ann's loving comforts were enlisted. Nicholas Munro Morgan arrived October 10, 1967. After full post-natal care, the little trio returned to Sacramento. Their newly designed lives with American-born Nicholas went well with many family visits enjoyed by all of us for the next year and more.

Dan's unforgiving physical ailments finally caused his death in September, 1969. With grieving reluctance, Jennifer took Nicholas back to England to the loving solace and care of his maternal grandparents, Olive and Ivan Wilby. Sadly, by the year's end, Susan Baker also passed away.

Following each of their extreme losses, a comforting closeness opened the hearts of Jennifer Morgan and David Baker. They were married December 20, 1970, at Diss Registry Office by Jennifer's father Ivan, a qualified registrar of marriages for South Norfolk, England. That event was of hallowed consequence, not only to the Baker and Wilby families, but its deeply seeded purity of purpose brought about profound approval and a host of pleasures to all of the Morgan clan.

Emma Louise Ingram Baker was born at Ipswich, Suffolk on September 1, 1972. She attended the Convent of Jesus and Mary, Thomas Mills School and Suffolk College, Ipswich. In womanhood, she has gone forward, not only in the workplace and practicing her artistic bent, but with entitlement as *Special Granddaughter Number Six* on the list of Wendy's and my roster of cherished grandchildren.

"Dear Nicholas," as we doting grandparents like to remember him, now approaching 30 years of age, holds a masters degree in English and Linguistics. He is now employed as lecturer at South Kent College, Folkstone. Also, Nicholas' "touch" with poem and prose provides him with a select branch on the spreading "family tree."

The marital vows taken by David and Jennifer nearly 27 years ago comprised a union blessed by the Lord in many ways. Their resolve came as a blessing to their counterpart Morgans, so far away in the western hemisphere. Their care in rearing Nicholas is an emblem of esteem to his American grandparents.

The David Baker family: Jennifer,
Emma, Nicholas and David

DANIEL MUNRO MORGAN
Staff Sergeant U.S.A.F.

Oh Danny Boy

Life came to me in Autumn time
Engendered by God's own design.
My parents dreamed my human being;
First born was I, new to their scene.

Those cuddling hours, those scented days,
Momentous love cast by Mother's ways;
The precious weeks grew on and on,
My family part became the bond.

The bloom of childhood dawned with zest,
Each new adventure became the best,
Those flavored times with pie-crust dough
And family meets at hearth's warm glow.

Life was so rich, so full, so fair.
Meantime insidious trouble flared.
My body born so clean, so pure,
Evil claims beset me to endure.
The while I drank the cup of life,
Too often nagging ills bore strife.

Hail boyhood days, to me, just flew.
Contentment was my vivid view,
A willing hand in the family scheme,
Serious thoughts seemed my natural theme.

My physique groaned from inward rife,
Which to me appeared as part of life.
Maturity, the experts claimed,
Would rid me of my life-long blame.
Challenges of manhood quickly came
And brought to me new heights to claim.
From school to Air Force was my change,
Engrossed was I with wonders strange.
The engines' roar, the quiet sky,
The quest for knowledge, the where, the why.

Those years my lonely life I led
Away from home and family thread.
But real adventure too I knew —
Those wondrous metal "birds" we flew
Were always talking back it seemed,
Trim of line, slim wings that gleamed.

The years went by, then England came;
That lovely land with sun and rain.
Who knew that she would be the place
Where I would meet my love, and trace
The trail of courtship's lovely ways
And matrimony's warm full days.

Then came God's blessing cute and sweet,
Babe Nicholas, for all to greet;
A miracle beyond compare
With winning smile and lungs to air.

Why must life wane at such a crucial hour
When need and hope demand my power?
But then my being was gnarled with trial;
Now I must rest and wait awhile.

I walk the Valley, you know where,
And take my vantage place up there,
To watch and hope and pray for all
Deeds circumspect, both large and small.
My loved ones all must fill the grail
Until Life's Ship has lost its sail.
Then will we meet again, I know,
To share the eternal afterglow.

Robert M. Morgan
November 1969

DEAR NICHOLAS

What was that jumping lithesome mite
That crossed before my eyes?
Not real, you say: no ordinary sight —
To me it's no surprise.
Perhaps some elf or widget ploy,
Yet, wait, why that's a knee-pant brown legged boy
Beckoned by some birdling lure
A sight I've seen a dozen times;
Dear Nicholas, to be sure !

But now I wonder, good Nicholas-One
Just how you really are.
I must confess, we miss you, Son,
When you're away so far.
Your Mom and Dad delight in you
With plans for play and school
I know you make them proud each day
With the things you say and do.

My, isn't being five just great
With six so close at hand.
Your Grandmother can barely wait
To view how straight you stand.
Each passing week our minds employ
All sorts of wishful schemes
By which we can renew our bond
With you, Dear Nicholas boy.

And now until that pleasant day
When we can see your smile,
Have fun, be kind and helpful, too,
To Sister, Mom and Dad, and all the while
You may be sure, Dear Nicholas, we love you.

Grandmother and Grandfather Morgan
1973

JOHN'S FAMILY

John Wesley Morgan, born October 28, 1941, arrived at 11:00 p.m. that unusual night of unrelated events. After two weeks of night-time "Dale Carnegie Sales Training," I received my graduation credentials about 9:30 p.m., just in time to rush from Portland's West Hills to its east side Emmanual Hospital to congratulate Lucy on our newborn second son. Moving on city streets that night was not easy, as the first trial "blackout" took effect in preparedness for the eventualities of then impending World War II.

Through adolescence, John's early years must all be labeled as inventive, singular and surprising. What other ten-year-old would locate a standing hollow cottonwood tree in our farm wooded area, move in several household articles, including bedding and food, and then settle in with "summer hours" for his interpretations of living alone in his little creative world? A tree-house, twenty feet above ground in another area on our farm, was naturally built and furnished by John, then age twelve. John's somewhat different teen years passed, much to his Mother's relief, and he became a man after he signed on with the United States Air Force.

Although described elsewhere in this general text, my father, Newton Elmer Morgan, died in January of 1963 at his home in Hemet, California, twelve hundred miles from our McMinnville, Oregon home. John, then stationed at Edwards Air Force Base near Lancaster, California, took over with great dignity and effectiveness. Tending to every funeral detail to the relief of his step-grandmother Margaret Matilda Morgan.

John married Danielle Ellen LeVigne on August 1, 1968. She and John lived variously in Rockford, Illinois; Houston, Texas; Portland, Oregon; Colorado Springs, Colorado;

and Simi Valley, California.

Their firstborn was Jacqueline Lee, arriving March 30, 1969. Always proper and petite, she was blessed with studious qualities and feminine pluses that have meted her an exciting, productive life as she eagerly looks toward matrimony in its finest form.

Victoria Anne, born May 25, 1970, had that certain sweetness, always a joy to her grandparents. She is now the mother of our first two great-grandchildren, Nicolle and Vincent. Always industrious and caring, Victoria has fashioned a comfortable lifestyle for her precious babies.

Matthew Munro Morgan was born on October 29, 1974. A boy of smiles, he was the final member of John and Danielle's blossoming family. Matthew, a self-made musician and band member, is now studying at Humbolt State University, and plans to teach following his graduation.

The John Morgan family: Danielle, Jacqueline, Victoria, John, and Matthew (in front)

TO JACQUELINE
OUR FIRST GRANDDAUGHTER

My life's been full of the pleasant things
That people say and do.
You can't believe the joy it brings to
Having a granddaughter such as you.

Our forbearers worked hard everyday
To build and live secure.
It's clear to me your chosen way
Has designs that will surely endure.

Your direct and positive sense of right
Brings joy to your Grandmother and me.
We endorse your willingness to fight
For the goals you've chosen to see.

Like all of our Clan, we're behind you, dear girl,
As life's great things unfold.
With spirit like yours, you'll join the whirl;
"Can do" and zest fit the Jacqueline mold.

Love from your Morgan Grandparents
Robert M. Morgan ~ March 15, 1986

MARY ANN'S FAMILY

Mary Ann Morgan Brenan, born September 19, 1944, understandably the apple of her father's eye, was a lovely recipient of so many of her mother's affable characteristics. She also most easily inherited certain of the fine traits of both my mother, Bessie Mae, and those of her Aunt Dorothy Munro Johnson, Bessie's sister.

Lucy and I gratifyingly watched Mary Ann form her future, comfortably supporting her lifestyle as she gathered business acumen. First gaining suitable knowledge of stenographics, then "Front Office" secretarial aplomb that brought her many friends and employers of lasting good fellowship, she flourished in the business world.

Her social acquaintances came and went, yet her inherent desire for the romantic door to open led to a chance introduction and her "dream marriage." Quite casually, she met the man who represented every aspect of her youthful prerequisites, John Richard Brenan, suitor personified.

With prime planning and all of the social whirls leading up to that cherished time-of-all-times, they were married April 22, 1978 as she had wished, in the living room of our Glendora home. Following the wedding and ensuing garden party, planned to the finest detail, Mary Ann and John properly bid all of the well-wishers a warm goodbye as she was swept away to a waiting world of comfort, care and splendor.

Ryan Christopher Brenan, born May 5, 1974, John Brenan's son by a former marriage, is easily identified in all of the family pictures. He's the one with a genuine smile from infancy, through adolescence, and into manhood, foretelling a rooted personality that will elevate him to a full, useful life, ready for all eventualities.

Michael Robert Brenan is a welcome addition to our roster of five grandsons. Born February 18, 1979, he is an exemplary bearer of youthful good manners and athletic prowess.

Colleen Elizabeth Brenan, making number five in our list of cherished granddaughters, arrived June 30, 1981, notably the first girl to be greeted by the Brenan family in one hundred thirty years. She quickly advanced through adolescence, emerging as a shining example of a brilliant young woman of many talents.

The John Brenan and Mary Ann Morgan Brenan family: Ryan, John and Mary Ann (in back); Michael and Colleen (in front)

MY HYDE PARK LAD ~
OUR FIRST BRENAN-MORGAN GRANDSON

This Boy I know has a wondrous smile
His Grandfather loves to see;
It's worth gold stacked high in a pile
And connotes a heart of glee.
I've known him from the very start;
My, my, how he does grow.
He's one who always does his part,
A trait we all should know.

This Lad comes from some good sound stock
Way back down through the years;
He's number one kid on the block
With lots of fun and few tears.
Growing up is hard to do,
But M.R.B. is in command.
I have no doubt and I'm sure, nor you,
That he'll grow strong and do
Right well for the Brenan band.

He studies hard and earns good marks,
And reading is a joy;
He's hitting baseballs in the parks,
That's Michael Robert boy.
He looks good with a basketball
And now he rides his bike;
Who knows what he'll do by Fall,
He's Grandad's God-Child tyke.

Robert M. Morgan ~ Spring 1987

JIM'S FAMILY

James Wendell Morgan, born September 17, 1947, entered our family as the last sibling. His infant viewpoint portrayed to him a common fireside environment steeped in motherly love, taunted some by his older brothers, but adored by his doting sister. And he grew, always athletic, and striving to excel.

He joined the United States Marine Corps, serving honorably in the ill-defined, cruel Vietnam War of horrors and desolation. Returning after two years of rigorous duty, feeling so strongly for the war wrongs dealt the Vietnam natives, he was obliged to do much soul-searching to keep from re-enlisting for a humanitarian second "hitch."

As a seasoned former Marine, Jim easily fit into the regulated business world, and the years advanced. During Jim's teen years before and after his military service, our family home on Richardson Lane in Glendora was situated across the street from the Neuenschwander home. By a stroke of good fortune, it was beautifully ensconced with a most attractive bevy of lovely daughters. With some gentle urging, Jim finally took careful note of that singular daughter who was just right for him. Anne Neuenschwander and James Wendell Morgan were married on July 26, 1969. It was a cherished ceremony performed by Anne's Grandfather Crampton.

A fond delight to Jim and Anne was the arrival of their firstborn, Amy Christine Morgan on February 2, 1974. Next born was cute Allison Lynne Morgan, destined to have an unusual charm, June 6, 1976. Their family gender balance started with the August 16, 1979 arrival of Christopher James Morgan. Jason Robert Morgan arrived on a most stormy night, November 16, 1980, his Morgan grandparents remember vividly. Thus was added another boy to complete the family which has contributed admirably to the Morgan name.

It is generally agreed that when grandparents remark about granddaughters, superlatives, exclamations of adoration and multiple synonyms for charm sometimes overwhelm the attentive reader.

I must be patiently exonerated when I describe my feelings for our third-in-line granddaughter Amy Christine Morgan Gunn. Amy's sweet impish smile has bewitched the Morgan Clan since the day she left the maternity ward. As she blossomed into womanhood, her prerequisites for a lifelong mate must have somehow been bequeathed to her by our Heavenly Father.

She was married at a lovely garden ceremony on August 19th, 1995 to James Avery Gunn, initiating and sealing one of the decade's most intricately lovable unions our family had the pleasure of enjoying. Amy is our first granddaughter to embark in the joys of matrimony.

She chose a man in James who suits Amy in a pattern likened to a fine original oil painting. Industrious, intelligent, likeable James now attends the University of Utah's School of Engineering, earning a 3.98 grade point average. He embodies all of the traits a grandfather-in-law wishes for a choice granddaughter. It will be these grandparents' pleasure to see this couple bloom.

The James Morgan family: James, Christopher, Amy, Allison, Jason, and Anne

TWELVE DAYS OF CHRISTMAS
THE MARCILE MORGAN'S WAY

Christmas spirit filled the air
That sharp December night.
The front chime sounded and from my chair
To the door I quickly sped
To find before my startled sight
A gaily done-up loaf of bread,
Hot from the hearth, it smelled divine,
Just right for sandwiches and toast at Santa time.

It must have been a yuletide Elf,
Or possibly a Christmas Sprite
To deftly place this toothsome part,
Then vanish in the winter dark,
But not before by written mark,
Forewarn of yet more gifts of some
Exciting Christmas bit to come.

And so it happened, eve on eve,
A gorgeous plant, more savory bits;
It seemed no gastronome reprieve
As we delighted in each ribboned kit.
Though I tried hard to see our donor,
Dashed out the door and round the corner;
Always like a fleeting bee
That Elf, or such, deprived my right to see
What sort of cloak, what color hair,
The likes of which seemed never there.

With gift on gift, right from the heart.
Perchance the seed of our invention,
Now we know how cute your part
In rounding out Christ-like convention;
No truer thought than family love
With the guidance of His hand above.

Jim Morgan's band, each of you,
Sure showed real zest.
With your nice tricks, a spritely crew
Vexed us; you were the best.
We won't forget your heartfelt pranks;
Grandfolks are pleased and full of THANKS.

Robert M. Morgan
December 26th, 1982
Describing the four Morgan children,
all under the age of 10,
sneaking gifts onto their grandparents' doorstep
12 nights in a row.

"CUZZIE" ~ Cousin Betty

No person other than each of her children, her two brothers, or me has crafted more genuine closeness to Lucy Ann (Wendy) than has "Cuzzie," her cousin Beatrice Stauss. Betty, as she is mostly known, beyond her many qualities, was destined to grow up a child of a broken home. The daughter of Amy and Ernest Hyland, from age two she resided comfortably in the old family home on Portland's East 23rd Street near East Hawthorne Avenue with her mother and her grandparents, Lillia and August Gerstel, fondly known to the family as "Popsi."

As early as age four, Betty spent her summers in Eugene with her father, Ernest Hyland. The large Hyland clan often shared Betty with other family members, but mostly with Estelle Poill. Aunt "Stella," as she was called, dutifully and with loving foster full-time care also kept Lucy Ann, following the untimely death of each of her parents. During those summers at Aunt Stella's shared home, the two cousins, Betty and Lucy Ann, developed a lasting bond, referring to each other with the shared nickname of Cuzzie.

Betty blossomed into womanhood and pursued her education at Oregon State Univeristy (then OSC). There she was taken with the handsome charm of another student, Ira Stauss. They were married December 26, 1943, in our Portland Eastmoreland home. Ira had just completed Midshipmen's School *en route* to over two years of active duty in the war-torn Pacific Theater with the United States Navy.

During Ira's absence, we welcomed Betty to live with us until mid-1945 when Ira returned for a two-month shore leave. The war ended, and Ira was honorably discharged from the Navy in time to welcome their firstborn child, daughter Irene Linda, on May 11, 1946. Her birth led to complications for Betty that again accorded her our home and cousin Lucy Ann's comforting ways.

Two sons followed for Betty and Ira. Randall Hyland was born on August 3, 1947, and John Damon arrived on March 30, 1953. The young family moved successively from Portland to Hillsboro and then permanently to Corvallis in 1958.

The two Cuzzies, close as they had become, nurtured their young with proper care. In the process, they created innumerable group gatherings, holiday dinners and other events that stimulated the several cousins to enjoy countless good times, almost always garnished with the best of toothsome meals. For more than seven decades, since that first shared summer, the Cuzzies' efforts ending with goodbyes always did and still do bring forth a "let's get together again soon."

Above: Lucy Ann Morgan and Beatrice Hyland Stauss, 1997; right: Beatrice and Lucy Ann with their daughters Irene and Mary Ann, 1947

COUSINS

It is my open wish that everyone places much the same loving association upon their cousins as I do. Cousins are such a part of each of our lives. Certainly as I look back to the earliest times in my life, cousins were close by, their lives somewhat intertwined with mine. As this entire work is an autobiography, historical acknowledgment of my cousins is noted here.

James Winfred Copeland, married to Elizabeth Mae Rinehart, is the eldest son of my Aunt Luella Eva Copeland. They have five sons. His sister, June Sarah Tillman, divorced, is the proud mother of five sons and one daughter, Anita. Winfred Scott Copeland, last child of my Aunt Luella is married to Anita Swartz. They have one daughter, Karen Sue.

Donald Demke, deceased, was an adopted son of my Aunt Daisey, married to Albert Demke.

Morgan Vernon Jeffcott, deceased, married to Mildred Cade, was the only son of my Aunt Nettie Jeffcott. Morgan and Mildred had a daughter, Doris June, and two sons.

Barbara Johnson Stewart married Jack Stewart and they had two children. She was the eldest child of my Aunt Dorothy Munro Johnson. Thomas Johnson was Dorothy's only son.

Alma Rita Kurtz, deceased, married to Joseph Woodle, was the daughter of my Aunt Mina Morgan Kurtz. Aunt Mina's son, Roy E. Kurtz, deceased, married and had three children.

William Kay Morgan, deceased, eldest son of my Uncle Alba Ralph Morgan, was married to Norma Kathrine Naylor. They had one daughter, Joyce Eleanor. Norma later married Bud Schluter. Richard A. Morgan, youngest son of my Uncle Alba, is unmarried.

Helen Elizabeth Spencer, deceased, bore two sons by her first marriage to Thomas J. Mahoney, Jr. She then married William Blitz. She was the daughter of my aunt Laura Violet Spencer.

John (Jack) Alfred Spencer, deceased, was my Aunt Laura's eldest son. Omar Corwin Spencer, Jr., deceased, Aunt Laura's youngest son, was married to Phyllis Rudeen. They had two daughters, Laurie Ann and Susan.

Sarah and W.H.H. Morgan and their children.
(Standing in back, left to right:)
Nellie, Mina, Alba, Daisy and Luella
(Seated, in middle:)
Sarah, W.H.H. and Nettie
(In front:)
Laura and Newton
(Photo courtesy of June Tillman)

SOMETHING OF A SAUVIE ISLAND LIFE

[The following four articles by Robert M. Morgan are reprinted with permission from The Sauvie Island Outlook, edited by Jean Fears]

Although that segment of the past has long since come and gone, an all-important part of everyday Sauvie Island farm life came to an unheralded end more than a brief five decades ago in 1941 when her tired old bones, all she had left, were burned on the mainland banks at the mouth of the Willamette River.

Who was "she"? Why, the trim, gleaming white little propeller steamer *America* that became so much a part of all of us who lived (by present day standards) so remotely on "The Island"a short ten-to-fifteen miles, as the crow flies, from teeming downtown Portland, Oregon.

During the first presidential term of Franklin Delano Roosevelt, in the year 1933, only a few Sauvie Island families near the Burlington Ferry landing had electricity and telephones. Before 1930, motor trucks were rarely seen on the island more than three miles from the ferry landing.

Life on "The Island," surrounded by the waters of the Columbia and Willamette Rivers and the Multnomah Channel, was dependent upon the steamer *America*. Island folks eagerly anticipated each of her arrivals as she served river and slough farm landings for over 20 years from 1912 into the 1930's.

Steamer *America* was not elegant as were so many of the stately sternwheel steamboats of Oregon history, such as the glamorous packets of three generations ago. *Hassalo, Harvest Queen, Lurline, Undine* and *Bailey Gatzert* were the finest. *America* was just part of our everyday lives.

On her river run, she left the city of St. Helens each morning at an early hour, stopping at each farm landing, some distance upstream from Warrior Rock. Her stops included many family names: Richardson, Johnson, Reeder, Hutchinson, McIntire, Browning, Copeland, Morgan, Cehloha, Gillihan, Lerch, Cashdollar and Hammond. Farm landings on the Columbia's Washington side (Waite, Stutzer and Scheruble) were reliably served, too. *America's* docking point in Portland was, for many years, at the foot of West Alder Street, just downstream from the old Burnside Bridge.

Something more needs to be recorded about boarding and riding on the steamer *America*. Mostly, that is, from the viewpoint of the far-away memories of a nine-year-old boy who eagerly anticipated those infrequent boat trips to Portland. It was nothing short of exhilarating waiting on the windswept dock of Morgan's Landing Farm on a cold, wet winter morning for *America's* quiet, generally reliable arrival about 9:00 a.m. From about a quarter-mile downstream, the Captain always signaled *America's* arrival by blowing the steam whistle one blast. The boat then slipped easily into the docking area.

The deck crew's first mate cried out, "Got a line, Sir!" A deck-hand slung the heavy inch-and-one-half hemp hawser around a dock piling to secure the boat's position for putting out the 14-inch-wide gangplank. Two or three hands would scramble ashore, returning aboard up the plank carrying two ten-gallon cans of milk. Once the milk cans were loaded, then the passengers went aboard. To that nine-year-old boy, stepping onto *America's* bow deck meant entering a welcome, different environment. The forward main deck house freight doors were always open at loading time. Immediately inside was the huge, oil-fired steam boiler, its oil fire giving off a steady growl, emitting a blast of warming, hot air. The smell of high pressure steam also added zest to the rumbling surroundings.

The boy bounded up the gangway to the second deck. The first stop was the men's forward cabin, which was spartan in appearance and permanently tainted with stale pipe and cigar smoke. A quick stop at the purser's office to pay the 50-cent fare then freed the boy to make his planned boat inspection. One of the two main attractions was the main-deck engine room just aft of the boiler. He would stand enraptured by the steady quiet pulse of the gleaming double-expansion, 100-horsepower vertical steam engine that powered *America* at an acceptable 12 knots, once underway. Percy, the slightly rotund engineer, always bedecked in laundered bib-overalls, was affable and friendly to the boy.

After greeting Percy in the enchanting engine room, the next place of intrigue was three decks up to the pilot house, a somewhat off-limits sanctuary. Always a cherished goal, it was approached with a measure of juvenile trepidation. There, high above the water, one had a commanding panoramic view of the river and its varied surroundings. A sort of official aura prevailed from just being there in that quiet sanctity. Captain Ring, who did not much take to nine-year-old boys, was largely non-conversant. He gently turned the huge steering wheel, first to the left and then right, to maintain his course as the wind and current presented constant challenges.

Those occasional, exciting days were the ultimate for this young boy who fondly recalls the 92-ton, 105-foot long propeller steamer *America*, originally built at Portland in 1889 by John G. Sound, master carpenter. She was rebuilt at Rainier, Oregon for Herbert Holman, owner of America Transportation Company. Mr. Holman and his boat were an important part of the Sauvie Island past, certainly worth remembering.

ABOUT WILD BLACKBERRIES

One would have to presume that just about everybody likes Wild Blackberry Jam. It is just a simple fact that when spread heavily on hot buttered toast or ladled generously over homemade vanilla ice cream, it comes very close to the utopia of epicurean delights. Of course, please don't allow your thoughts to pass by that apex of all desserts, Wild Blackberry Pie, the way you remember the likes of Grandmother, Aunt Belle and dear old Mom baked it.

Quite a few things must be said about blackberries. Some very luscious plant varieties such as Northwest, Boysen and Pacific, have been bred by botanists back through the ages. Those patent varieties had special flavors and aromas closely rivaling true Sauvie Island Wild Blackberries, but never quite equaling the true essence of that native bramble plant. The record must be kept clear about Wild Blackberries as they still grow on Sauvie Island, but not (of course!) in the profusion with which they flourished in the early days of natural low-land flooding before the great island dikes were built. The novice berry picker often confuses Evergreens and Himalayas that grow commonly wild in fence rows and thickets almost everywhere in Western Oregon and Washington. Although flavorsome and pleasant, these two errant fruit-bearing rose-bramble clan members fall way short of the true Sauvie Island Wild Blackberry in sauce, jell or tarts.

After some nostalgic reminiscences of jam-making aromas floating away from the extra summer heat of Mother's wood-burning kitchen stove, perhaps the fondest memories of all come to mind about picking Wild Blackberries in the Island setting. First of all, these jewels of the cottonwood thickets were always at their savory best just as the floodwaters receded from the ridge areas where they ripened to their elegant best about the first of July. Sometimes Dad even had to use the rowboat to get to certain ridges where he knew the berries would be biggest. Secondly, with the receding flood waters, a perfect habitat was left for the carnivorous hoards of mosquitos that lay in wait to attack the poorly clad would-be picker. Dad knew best, though. He wore a cheesecloth veil drooping down over his neck and face, worn under the old felt hat. Long sleeves and old gloves with the finger-ends cut out gave him basic protection. Then there was his pipe; mosquitos never liked tobacco smoke. Thirdly, a distinct difference existed in the vines amongst these noble gems of the ridge land's underbrush. Dad knew and soon taught me to watch for a hardy, heavy stalk, and with not quite so dense foliage. That was where those three-quarter-inch black beauties hung, waiting to grace the interior of the one-gallon lard picking pail. The bail of the pail was intersected by a tight rope tied around the waist, thereby allowing both hands to be free, one holding a two-foot-long stick for parting the vines, the other to do the picking.

When picking was at its delightful best, the waist-held lard pail filled quickly. Usually, from the ubiquitous dairy room at the farm, two of those gleaming nickel-plated three-gallon milk pails would be temporarily borrowed for the day's picking. Placed at a central point, into them went lard pailful after pailful. It was not uncommon for two experienced pickers to pick five or six gallons of that never-to-be-equaled fruit in two or three hours. Always having been one to relish good food, I guess some of my fondest early childhood memories are the sight of Dad coming up the walk to the farm house in the summer carrying two brimming milk buckets full of fragrant Wild Blackberries. On the other side of the memory coin is winter, seeing him trudging up the same path with a half-dozen fat Mallard ducks, knowing full well what the end-point would be, dressed and stuffed for the oven, and thence onto the dining room table.

More can be said about *rosaceae rubus*, the broad family berry name including Sauvie Island Wild Blackberries, not to be confused with second best upland Wild Black-berries. Alas, without even a quart jar full as testimonial proof of what's been said, how could I, over one thousand miles from the Island's succulent source, ever prove my points to the uninitiated.

THE SAUVIE ISLAND LINK

Sauvie Island, so much a part of my life, originally known as *Wapato* by the local Indian tribes, was first seen by Lieutenant Broughton in 1792. It would be 158 years of historic progress before a bridge would link the Island to the mainland. I have detailed much about the halcyon days of water transportation in and around Portland, Oregon. An excerpt from my writing about the "Ferry Days" is as follows.

"It was a pleasant, unhurried world, it seemed, when my father first purchased the new 1925 Essex car. Now we could drive to Portland and return in a couple of hours, as compared to riding the steamer *America*, consuming most of one whole day. Even though the city was only fifteen miles away from Morgan's Landing Farm, the car trip was quite a feat, particularly in the winter, for there were no roads for the first three miles. Leaving the farm, we would head west out across the meadows and mud flats. Seven gates later, we would emerge from the foot-deep ruts unto a graveled county road, leaving the last gate behind. Then we could take the tire chains off, and breeze along at thirty miles per hour, soon reaching actual pavement for the last four miles to the Burlington Ferry landing. After a short wait, we then crossed the Multnomah Channel, continuing along the mainland trestle, over the S.P.&S. Railroad tracks, up the very steep hill to Burlington, and thence onto the nicely paved Highway #30 and quickly into Linnton, St. Johns or the big City."

Several craft, from a very early crude barge to the last fine steel-hulled *Sauvie Island*, commissioned in 1935, served the Islanders as they crossed to the mainland until the heralded new bridge was opened December 30, 1950.

Much acclaim was accorded the anticipated opening of the Sauve Island Bridge, a Multnomah County funded and managed structure, the framework of which was largely built of reclaimed, useable steel from the old Burnside Bridge. The old Burnside was replaced by the present structure in 1926. The Sauvie Island Grange, with its pre-eminence as the community center, formed committees to develop a dedication program. I was selected as the Bridge Dedication Chairman.

When the big day arrived, the Oregon State Highway Commission, state engineer E. H. Baldock, together with the bridge designer Ellsworth Rickets, were present for the dedication ceremony. A dedication address was given by the honorable Douglas McKay, Governor of Oregon, adding much importance to the occasion. The ceremonial Ribbon Cutting staged to formally open the bridge was performed by Mrs. J. W. Frazer, elderly mother of Governor McKay, and matriarch of one of the first pioneer Island families.

Following the opening of the bridge, after much fanfare, flowers and music, a motorcade loaded with community spirit toured the Island, celebrating the bridge as a symbol of the Island's connection to the outside world, at last.

REFLECTIONS OF A NATIVE SON

I am a son of the Great River of the West, where flows the Oregon, the mighty Columbia River, water artery through the ages from the northern reaches of the Selkirks, Kootenais and Nelson Range to the Pacific Ocean.

Child of the river, raised on her shores, I know her history and her moods. I saw her vent her massive fury in the flood of the Century, May 30, 1948. Her waters, in excess of 1,300,000 cubic feet per second, crowded the overtaxed spillways of Bonneville Dam. Such monstrous torrents could submerge the state of North Dakota over three feet deep in one day.

I have ridden the bosom of her crest in the halcyon, waning days of steam navigation when the majestic sternwheel steamboats plied her waters. Their smokestacks trailed cloud-white plumes of exhaust steam over their wakes in a colorful page of history.

She has drowsed in winter slumber under a rigid ice pack blanket, shore to shore, so thick as to allow an automobile to be driven across her breadth from Oregon to Washington at Vancouver, circa 1930.

From beyond the millennium, she nurtured the tribes of native American Indians, providing nutritious salmon and sturgeon. Her seasonal floods replenishing bottom lands with rich silt, creating a habitat for the healthy growth of the cottonwood, wild berries, rich green grasses and the Wapato, a native form of potato.

Since the winter of 1805, when she bore the Lewis and Clark Expedition to their winter encampment, which later became Fort Astoria, the Columbia River has served as an avenue of commerce. Merchant sailing vessels and the Hudson's Bay Company's first steamboat, *Beaver*, carried the trade upon her ever-ample waters to and from Fort

Vancouver from 1825.

I saw her yield her stupendous power to the accomplishments of modern engineering with the building of the Grand Coulee Dam, started in 1933, the greatest concrete monolith of the time. So effective was the harnessing of her massive flows, transformed to hydro-electric energy at Bonneville and Grand Coulee, her latent strength brought victory to the Allied Powers of World War II much sooner. The generation of electric power from her waters provided a generous amount of Northwest electricity to allow the extraction of lightweight aluminum from bauxite ore. The process supplied never-before-imagined quantities of that metal to produce droves of fighter aircraft which summarily crushed the German foe.

Her waters and those of her tributary, the picturesque Willamette, were disparaged and degraded after the turn of this century by uncontrolled dumping of municipal and commercial sewage. Efforts of civic, government and private agencies have now, these many years later, transformed those native waters back to clean, tertiary-treated streams that host an ever expanding recreational use in a model environment.

It is with an expression of fondness and pride that I liken my relationship to the greatest of all Western rivers. No wonder I am proud to relate her majestic way, where flows the Oregon, the Columbia River.

A LETTER TO MY SONS

September 14, 1976

Dear John and Jim:

This letter is, of course, long overdue. Because of matters of the heart, it was not, somehow, quite possible for me to do this sooner.

September for all these years has been a happy "Birthday Month" as three of our immediate family for so many years celebrated "their days." More recently, the tragedy of Dan's death date has marred the happiness of this month, if not openly, certainly individually and surely secretly, with some of us.

Although it is not pleasant to recall, I must now review the fateful day of September 27, 1969. Mother and I had been away on an overnight holiday, returning to Dan's and Jenny's presumably for a happy reunion and Sunday dinner with the family, only to sense that something was wrong, as we stepped from the car to approach the front door of their apartment. And then, upon entering, to learn the massive burden that you two shared as you waited for our return.

As one learns to walk with Christ, the spirited buttress holds you up to impossible situations that are hard to accept. The heart, by contrast, heals terribly slowly of a loved one's loss.

Since that fateful day, I have felt indebted to you two for having to bear the burden of the moment when Mother and I appeared on that sad scene, after your many traumatic hours of trying to locate us.

I shall not, to my last day, forget the stalwart way in which you, John, the elder, backed up by you, Jim, the junior, told us in such a straight-forward way of Jenny and Nick's well-being and of Dan's passing away. Surely this is the kind of substance of which strong men are made and I have since that day been everlastingly grateful to have sons of such a foundation.

I trust that each of you will always convey to your families, and particularly your children, the same condition of frankness and sincerity with which you set yourselves apart on that sad, unforgettable Sunday.

With love,

Your father

THROUGH THE AVENUE OF YEARS
~ A DEDICATION TO OUR GRANDCHILDREN

Nicholas Munro Morgan-Baker
Born in America, reared in England. You, the first, just naturally marked a shining milepost as our immediate family began to expand into the third generation.

Jacqueline Lee Morgan
Grandmother's and my first Granddaughter, what a joy to welcome you. Always cute and pert were you. Your family moves kept us often separated. I did write a poem about you to express my thoughts.

Amy Christine Morgan
Our most cherished memories are of the many times through your growing years that you were with us. Grandmother was privileged, those early times that she was with you privately.

Victoria Anne Morgan
Your smile has transported you, so gracefully, in your Grandparents' esteem. We congratulate you for the substantial way you have fashioned a formulative life for Nicolle and Vincent.

Matthew Munro Morgan
Your superior performance in growing up as you have is one merit to your determination to achieve. We hope you will carry on in your precision in music.

Allison Lee Morgan
6/6/76, your birth date, is indelibly marked in your Morgan Grandfather's mind. A date to remember, as another budding Granddaughter has blessed us. Now, you're grown, for all the world, a charm.

Michael Robert Brenan
There never was any question about our "Hyde Park Lad" as my poem to you implies.

Christopher James Morgan
As a boy of many talents, I foresee you as a man of well-chosen words with a winsome smile accompanying your important ways.

Jason Robert Morgan

With a hand to fit a ball glove, a soccer toe and a willful desire to win, the pages of life will turn easily for you.

Colleen Elizabeth Brenan

A "Brenan" Granddaughter of historic distinction, you were born as the first girl in over 130 years, with much adoration and acclaim. Your character, so well defined in the true Brenan heritage, sets you apart in your Grandfather's eyes as a distinct, well-ordered individual.

Ryan Christopher Brenan

As a Grandson to us by your father's first marriage, you have never appeared to us as anything but 100 percent pure Brenan. We admire your affection for the Brenan side, your quizzical nature and your admirable physique, all of which will take you far.

Emma Louise Baker

It was the Morgan Clan's pleasant fortune when you, our unrelated English Granddaughter, cousin and niece were born and became a link from far across the world to further bind the "family" tie.

Robert Morgan, surrounded by grandchildren (top, left to right) Colleen Brenan (infant), Victoria Morgan, Ryan Brenan, Matthew Morgan, Amy Morgan and Jacqueline Morgan; (in front) Allison Morgan, Michael Brenan, Jason and Christopher Morgan. (Absent: Nicholas Morgan-Baker and Emma Baker)

I BELIEVE IN GRANDSONS

I do believe in Grandsons ~
Allow me to state my view.
Credit them with good minds and hands,
Future's stake for me and for you.
I have seen enough to take my stand
Each one has hopes and wants untold,
Guiding each Lad to become a man,
Our task is helping to form the mold.

Do you know things about Grandsons?
I can list quite a few;
Wonders to do with ants and butterflies.
Their excitement with kites that they flew,
And secret thoughts about Superman,
Super Dad ranks most high.
The formative years of parents' kind hands,
The youthful quest for security's tie.

Please never forget about Grandsons.
They are precious to us all.
Our charges and our chosen ones
While each is growing tall.
In infancy they're like young cubs,
No cares to weight them down,
Although they're prone to make some flubs,
Grandfathers only look away and frown.

I'll stake my all on Grandsons
In this difficult world of today,
A serious challenge they've begun
Including holding diversions at bay.
Their ties are family, church, country and school;
Oldsters buttress their lives with experiences past
To help them in society's turbulent pool
With a firm foundation that lasts.

An easy choice is with Grandsons.
One could be big leaguer on the pitcher's mound,
Yet another a wide receiver;
I know one whose talents abound,
They all have me hooked ~ I'm a believer.
Another could be in a concert band.
One's personality tends towards entrepreneurial might,
The corporate ladder beckons the first in a distant land.

Now, best of all, each trusts our Father.
They have moral creeds they have learned.
Society's low ebbs are to them no bother.
Their Grandfather's respect justly earned.
Wholesome dreams have a place in life's plan
Plus myriad rewards rightly won.
You can be sure I'll do all I can
To assure victory comes to each Grandson.

Grandfather Bob Morgan ~ 1985-91

GLENEDEN BEACH CHRISTIAN CHURCH

When Lucy Ann and I established roots at Salishan in 1989, we soon found a Christian haven in non-affiliated Gleneden Beach Christian Church. Its people welcomed us warmly.

Perhaps the text of one verse from Samuel S. Wesley's fine old gospel hymn touches well our association with "The Church on the Hill."

> *Elect from every nation,*
> *Yet one o'er all the earth*
> *Her character of salvation,*
> *One Lord, one faith, one birth.*
>
> *One Holy name she blesses,*
> *Partakes one Holy food*
> *And to one hope she presses,*
> *With every grace endued.*

Edward E. Peery and Daydra L. Peery have been the thong that binds. Pastor Ed was unanimously voted in as Church Pastor on June 1, 1991. The couple's spiritual guidance and bounding energy were rewarding as the church group elders built, then dedicated the fine new chapel in September, 1993.

When Jennifer and David Baker last visited us at Salishan in 1994, surely their most memorable event here was being baptized with full immersion by Pastor Ed. Lucy Ann and I have enjoyed the company of the Peerys on certain "free time" for them when we have garnished our respective freezers with the bounties of Peach-Picking Picnics.

DEDICATION to the CHURCH ON THE HILL

"A rhapsody tones on a coastal hill.
Blessed music fills the air;
It's where the Lord displays His will
Through the people's care.

A body of believers, they
Who marked each meeting time;
His presence was there each sacred day,
Like the fruit from the lasting vine.

A church they built with caring hands
Afforded with gifts from afar and near.
It all was done on God's treasured land
For His church all held so dear.

Now a temple, crisp and new as it stands,
An elegant testimony, too,
Of the sweat and the love of a spiritual band
Comprised of a reverent few.

I sense the dawn is breaking,
I hear the Robin's trill.
It must mark a strong awakening
For His church, as it stands on a hill."

Robert M. Morgan, 1993
Re-printed with permission from the Dedication
Booklet, Gleneden Beach Christian Church

Bob and Lucy Ann Morgan, Daydra and Ed Peery

EARLY HISTORY OF THE FAMILY OF
EDWARD AND MARY MORGAN
Researched and written by Gregory L. Nelson,
family historian and second cousin, twice removed

Edward Morgan (senior) was born in southern England, Sussex County, in the year 1787. He was married to a woman named Sarah in England and came to the United States when about thirty years old, around 1817. His first marriage produced three children: Thomas, and namesakes Sarah and Edward Morgan. It is not clear whether the children were born in England or in the United States. While living in England, Edward Morgan had been a shoemaker by trade, but after reaching Ohio and in subsequent years, he was a farmer.

After reaching the United States, he began residence in the state of Ohio, where his first wife Sarah died. On the 30th day of June, 1828, Edward Morgan was again married, to Mary Shirley in Hamilton County, Ohio. Mary Shirley was a native of Virginia. The following children were born to this marriage: Benjamin, Mary, Isabella, George, William, Julia Ann, Catherine, James and Lucinda. The names of these children are shown by an affidavit made by Edward Morgan dated the 14th day of November, 1853.

While the family originally lived in Ohio, they moved to Iowa where they lived for a year or so before migrating to the West in 1845, the third year of organized wagon trains.

We do not have too much information as to the trip of the Edward and Mary Morgan family across the plains and the mountains in 1845, arriving in Oregon on the 15th day of November. During that year, approximately 3,000 people migrated to the Oregon country, divided into companies of fifty or more per wagon train.

I do not know who the leader was of the particular wagon train which included the Edward and Mary Morgan family. It is assumed that they had at least one covered wagon. Since Edward Morgan was born in 1787, he was approximately fifty-eight years old when they crossed the plains.

Many of the children were young and some of them were probably born after they reached Oregon. However, sons Edward and Benjamin were boys or young men, probably under age twenty. Having departed in March, they took about eight months to make the crossing.

The year 1845 was an unusual year in the story of immigration to the West. That was the year in which Stephen H. L. Meek, a brother of Joe Meek, guided some immigrants on a new route and about 150 wagons followed him. The route proved to be unsatisfactory and there was much hardship and suffering, and some loss of life from his followers. Also in 1845, Samuel K. Barlow found a route or trail south of Mt. Hood which in time came to be followed from The Dalles to the Willamette Valley, rather than down the Columbia River. This was late in the season, and I believe that the Morgan family came down the Columbia river, which was the route followed by the main body of immigrants then.

Arriving in Oregon in 1845, the Morgan family lived in Washington County for a few years and then came to Sauvie Island. Their first year on the island, they lived on what is now Oak Island, where the racoons were so thick that the family had a hard time keeping itself supplied with food.

As of July 4, 1849, Edward and Mary Morgan took as their residence and eventually perfected their title on what was known as the Morgan Donation Land Claim located along the Columbia River. A large part of that claim still belongs to members of the family. When the Morgan

Donation Land Claim was settled, it is interesting that their first house was of hewed cottonwood logs, and that the family had two yoke of oxen and one cow.

Since Edward Morgan was a citizen of England when he came to this country, it became necessary for him to declare his intention and become a citizen of the United States. He filed his intention to become a citizen in Washington County in the territory of Oregon on the 4th day of November, 1851, and gave his final affidavit as to citizenship at Oregon City on the 24th day of July, 1854. He took his oath as a citizen of the United States on September 1, 1863. That oath of citizenship is a striking reminder of our duties as citizens of the United States today, and it bears repeating here:

I, EDWARD MORGAN, a donation Claimant of Multnomah Co. Oregon do solemnly swear that I will support, protect, and defend the Constitution and Government of the United States against all enemies, whether domestic or foreign, and that I will bear true faith, allegiance, and loyalty to the same, any ordinance, resolution, or law of any State Convention of Legislature to the contrary notwithstanding; and, further, that I do this with a full determination, pledge, and purpose, without any mental reservation or evasion whatsoever; and, further, that I will well and faithfully perform all the duties which may be required of me by law. So help me God.
(Signed) Edward Morgan

Edward Morgan completed his proof of residence on the Donation Land Claim and the certificate to that effect was issued to him under a date of November 30, 1863, the date of the commencement of such residence having been established in the official papers as July 4, 1849. He would continue to work the land until his death in 1872 at the age of 84. Mary Morgan died in 1875 at the age of sixty-six.

Members of the family of Edward and Mary Morgan may well be proud of their ancestry. It required considerable courage for Edward Morgan with his first wife and children to migrate from England to this country in the early 1800's because the United States at that time had just started on its course as a great nation. The pioneer spirit of Edward Morgan was best evidenced by the fact that he did not stop on the Atlantic coast, but came to the state of Ohio, which at that time was pretty far west. Then after losing his first wife and marrying a second, and having a large family of children, in the year 1845 he had the courage to cross the plains and the mountains to the Oregon country. This was a journey of great hardships, both while on the journey and after arriving here. The spirit of the pioneers with courage, good judgment and hard work characterizes Edward Morgan and has been exemplified down through the years by all of his descendants. It is the spirit which has made America strong and will keep it strong as long as men and women want their freedom and love a free country.

William and Sarah Morgan and grandchildren: (standing back row) James M. Copeland, Robert M. Morgan, John A. Spencer, William K. Morgan, Morgan Jeffcot; (middle row) Richard A. Morgan, W.H.H. Morgan, Sarah O. Morgan, Omar C. Spencer Jr.; (seated front row) Alma R. Kurtz, Winfred Copeland Jr., June S. Copeland, Donald Demke, Helen E. Spencer

BOATS OF THE COLUMBIA AND WILLAMETTE RIVERS
That I have Known in the Early 20ᵗʰ Century

My true interest, by association, with the daily comings and goings of the last of the many colorful passenger, freight and tow boats that plied the Columbia, Cowlitz, Snake and Willamette Rivers reached its crest in my adolescent mind in 1924 at age 11. At that historic date as river transportation began to fall to the advantages of railroads and highways, I could identify and name 67 steam, diesel, sternwheel and propeller boats. Their industrious progression through the years has been most colorful to me.

Recording statistical data for all of them became too much of a burden for me. Certain notations, however, seemed cognizant. In April, 1995, I gave the "Key Accounting of Statistics, Marine Record of Oregon 1850-1917" to the Oregon Historical Society as a permanent library artifact. That record contains viable details of the boats listed here.

AMERICA, *steam, screw, 94-foot, built in Portland in 1889, rebuilt twice, then 100-foot, end 1946;* ASTORIA, *steam, screw, end 1923;* ANNIE COMINGS, *steam, sternwheel, 1887-1941;* BEAVER, *steam, sternwheel, owned by Harkins then Shaver Transportation Company, end 1934;* CATHERINE, *steam, sternwheel;* CASCADES, *steam, sternwheel, built in 1882 for the US Corps of Engineers, rebuilt 1912, 500 hp, Shaver, over 52 years of service on the rivers;* CLAIRE, *steam, sternwheel, 716 hp, built 1918, Shaver;* C. MENNSINGER, *steam, sternwheel;* COWLITZ, *steam, sternwheel;* DALLES CITY, *steam, sternwheel, passenger, freight, packet;* DIAMOND O, *steam, sternwheel;* EFIN, *gasoline, screw, 60-foot, 90 hp;* ECHO, *diesel, screw, log boom tender, Shaver;* FLEETWOOD, *diesel, screw, passenger and freight;* F.B. JONES, *steam, sternwheel;* GREYHOUND, *steam, sternwheel, built 1924, 65-foot;* GAMECOCK, *steam, sternwheel, owned by F.B. Jones;* GEORGIANNA, *steam, screw, owned by Harkins;* GEORGIE BURTON, *steam, sternwheel, 1896, W.S. Bentley;* GRAHMONA, *steam, sternwheel, 700 hp, Willamette passenger packet;* GEORGE W. MENDELL, *steam, screw, 100-foot US Corps of Engineers survey boat;* HENDERSON, *steam, sternwheel, 1912, Shaver;* HARVEST QUEEN, *steam, sternwheel;* HERCULES, *steam, sternwheel, Staghound, end Big Eddy;* HUSTLER, *steam, sternwheel, 105-foot, 1891-1908, rebuilt;* HASSALO, *steam, sternwheel;* IMPERIAL, *diesel, screw;* INSTERSTATE, *steam, sternwheel, built 1918;* IONE, *steam, sternwheel, 141-foot, built 1908;* IRALDA, *steam, screw, built 1906, Port-Rainier passenger packet;* JESSIE HARKINS, *diesel, screw, 200 hp, (Pearl) Shaver;* J.N. TEALE, *steam, sternwheel, 1907, burned, rebuilt 1908;* J.K. WENTWORTH, *steam, sternwheel;* JEAN, *steam, sternwheel;* LA CENTER, *steam, sternwheel, burned wood, hauled cattle;* LEWISTON, *steam, sternwheel;* LURLINE, *steam, sternwheel, Port Astoria passenger packet;* LOGGER, *steam, sternwheel, fueled with "hog fuel;"* MADALINE, *steam, sternwheel, (Jos.Kellog);* MARIA, *steam, sternwheel;* MATHALOMA, *steam, sternwheel, US Corps of Engineers snag removal;* METLACO, *steam, sternwheel;* NESTER, *steam, sternwheel;* NORTHWESTERN, *steam, sternwheel;* N.R. LANG, *steam, sternwheel;* NO WONDER, *steam, sternwheel, Shaver;* OKLAHAMA, *steam, sternwheel;* POMONA, *steam, sternwheel, owned by Port-of-Portland;* PORTLAND, *steam, sternwheel, built in 1919, 185-foot, 1500 hp, rebuilt by the Oregon Maritime Center;* PRONTO, *steam, sternwheel, built 1881 (Manzanillo by F.B. Jones);* RELIEF, *steam, sternwheel;* ROBERT YOUNG, *steam, sternwheel;* SARAH DIXON, *steam, sternwheel, built 1892, rebuilt 1906;* SERVICE, *steam, sternwheel, 151-foot, built 1908, 600 hp;* SKAGIT CHIEF, *steam, sternwheel;* SKOOKUM, *steam, sternwheel;* SHAVER, *steam, sternwheel;* STRANGER, *steam, sternwheel;* TWIN CITIES, *steam, sternwheel, 155-foot, 600 hp;* T.J. POTTER, *steam, side-wheel, passenger packet (retired);* UMATILLA, *steam, sternwheel, 160-foot, built 1908, rebuilt 1928;* UNDINE, *steam, sternwheel, fast passenger and freight packet;* WAUNA, *steam, sternwheel;* WEONE, *steam, sternwheel.*

Lucy Ann Morgan, Queen of Hearts

QUEEN OF HEARTS

~ What does it take to be a Queen of Hearts
And then the Queen of Diamonds, too?
It takes someone with lots of attributes ~
I'd like to name a few. ~

~ You've no doubt seen sun scalloped clouds
Or scented morning's dew ~
Heard the carnival of happy crowds ~
Drunk in a sunset's hue. ~

~ Someone so very special that
Her virtues are without compare;
And just so that I may clear the air,
How fortunate was I that day
She chose to cast her lot my way. ~

~ She is so dear and kind and sweet to me
And knows the things that set men free.
She is God's own child and something more;
I should have said this, much before.
Her personal measures of balance comprise
A scope of life that seems so wise. ~

~ Even tempered ~ kind of hand,
She is my wife ~ and, understand,
Hard put am I to meet her pace
What with her mode and knowing grace.
Not often do you find this blend.
God grant our bliss will never end. ~

ABOUT THE AUTHOR

Author Robert M. Morgan
Courtesy of the Irrigation
Association

Robert Munro Morgan's Oregon family lineage dates back more than 150 years. His great-grandfather, Edward Morgan, and family trekked the Oregon Trail west to the then village of Linnton, Oregon Territory in 1845, the third year of organized wagon trains. With that inborn pioneer bearing, he inherited a strong sense of will toward his forbearer's endurance and the family persuasion to persevere.

Growing up as a part of the historic Sauvie Island acres known as Morgan's Landing Farm on the banks of the Columbia River provided a storehouse of formulation granted to only a select few progeny of the early twentieth century. His adolescence was filled with the wonders of farm machinery, the miracles of steam power, and an introduction to the earliest internal combustion marine diesel engines – all without the benefit or intrusion of either a radio or telephone to communicate with a life beyond his family's island farm community. These factors contributed to his unrelenting boyish attraction to river boating on The Great River of the West, and made an everlasting mark on his fertile imagination as he grew to manhood.

Pumps, pipes and power sources were industrial ingredients in the next stage of his life as husband, father and breadwinner. Beginning in the state of Oregon, his career path then took him along the West Coast, across the nation, and finally led him throughout the world in design and application of equipment to irrigate agricultural, recreational and residential developments.

Morgan has also served his profession for many decades through leadership roles in the American Society of Agricultural Engineers, the Irrigation Association, and his local Grange. His writings include authoring *Water and the Land*, a landmark work on irrigation history, and numerous articles in various professional journals and historical newsletters.

Now at home along the Oregon Coast in the select quietude of "Salishan" and its native beauty with his wife Lucy Ann "Wendy," he reviews with pride and gratitude his many years of invaluable professional experiences while reveling in the joys of a loving family, including twelve grandchildren and two great-grandchildren.

*Robert and Lucy Ann Morgan
appreciating the inspiring
ocean view in front of their
Gleneden Beach home
[artist: Randall H. Stauss]*